THE PROCESS OF PURPOSE
Michael Moss Ph.D.

Other books by Dr. Moss:

"SUCCESS POWER PRINCIPLES"

"Happiness is a Constant Choice"

"BLACK LOVE MATTERS: Black Love is a Superpower"
"African Spiritual Systems: The Origin of European Religions"
"Faith God & Power: It's All About You"

Email: MichaelMossM@aol.com

THE PROCESS OF PURPOSE

By

Michael Moss Ph.D.

SANKOFA PRESS

the
purpose
of life
is a
life of
purpose.
-robert byrne

Dedicated

To

Bishop Terence E. Coleman (T.C.)

Thanks T.C. (Bishop Coleman) for inspiring me to write this book with your comments on my Face Book page, in response to the post of my outline for my sermon, "The Process of Purpose". I followed your advice and, "put that in a book."

"That's awesome. You ought to put that in a book. Great work MOG. Well crafted. Speaking through your experiences going through the process." -- Bishop Terence E. Coleman (Comments from Face Book post.)

Nia
(Purpose)

TABLE OF CONTENTS

"Nothing will take the place of purpose. Talent is good, but nothing is more common than unsuccessful men of talent. Genius is good, but the man who has genius usually sits in the shade and admires it. Intellectual culture is good, but the country is full of unsuccessful educated men, and neither Washington nor Lincoln were of the schools. Favorable circumstances are not to be despised—with or without any or all of these you may have success, but never without purpose."

(Reverend M. M. Callen 1891)

PREFACE

Imagine a pill that would reduce cognitive decline (Alzheimer's disease) by 40-50%. Reduce macroscopic stroke by 40%. Aid sleep apnea. And add seven (7) years to your life. Decrease depression and give you a sense of fulfillment. Withstand pain better, have a healthier brain, and immunize you from vain living. Well, that "magic pill" is purpose.

Mark Twain stated, "The two most important days in your life are the day you are born, and the day you find out why." Myles Munroe stated, "The greatest tragedy in life is not death, but a life without a purpose." Oliver Wendell Holmes stated, "Most of us go to our graves with our music still inside us, un-played."

Purpose is absolutely fundamental to life. Purpose is the answer to the question, "Why". The "why" of a thing, is the reason for its creation. If you want to know the purpose or "why" for a thing, you must ask its creator. God gave Adam a purpose and a job, before He gave him a woman. His purpose was to be fruitful and multiply and reflect the image of God on earth, as it is in heaven. You can't produce anything by yourself, so God gave him help, in the form of a woman.

The result in multiplication is a product. Anything times itself, equals itself. In order to produce, we must enter into a relationship. Productivity is the result of a relationship of multiplication. The first not good in the Bible is, "It is not good for man to be alone." Why? Because you need to be in some type of relationship to have a productive life. So purpose is related to people.

Pablo Picasso stated, "The meaning of life is to find your gift. The purpose of life is to give it away." A life without purpose, as practiced in relationships, is a life without meaning.

Not only is a life without purpose without meaning, it is abusive. The great Myles Munroe stated that: "Where purpose is not known, abuse is inevitable." Abuse means "abnormal use". If you don't know your purpose, you will abuse yourself, and others will abuse and re-purpose you for their selfish use. Knowing your purpose is absolutely necessary.

Purpose Quotes

"The two most important days in your life are the day you are born and the day you find out why." —Mark Twain.

"Most of us go to our graves witch our music still inside us, unplayed." — Oliver Wendell Holmes

"The meaning of life is to find your gift. The purpose of life is to give it away." —Pablo Picasso

"If you want to find your true purpose in life, know this for certain: Your purpose will only be found in service to others, and in being connected to something far greater than your body/mind/ego." - Dr. Wayne Dyer

"The greatest tragedy in life is not death, but a life without a purpose."
— Myles Munroe

Let us hear the conclusion of the whole matter: Fear God, and keep his commandments: for this is the whole duty of man. (Ecclesiastes 12:13)

Great minds have purpose, little minds have wishes. ---- Michael Moss

A Purpose driven person is never bored, they always have something to do. --- Michael Moss

Purpose is the impulse of life. --- Michael Moss

God has a purpose for your pain.
A reason for your struggle.
And a reward for your faithfulness.

Plan with a Purpose
Prepare with a Prayer
Proceed with Positivity
Pursue with Persistence
(African Proverb)

"I've learned that people will forget what you said, people will forget what you did, but people will never forget how you made them feel." ---Maya Angelou

"You may not control all the events that happen to you, but you can decide not to be reduced by them. Try to be a rainbow in someone else's cloud. Do not complain. Make every effort to change things you do not like. If you cannot make a change, change the way you have been thinking. You might find a new solution." ---Maya Angelou

Life isn't about surviving but about thriving. ---Maya Angelou

"My mission in life is not merely to survive, but to thrive; and to do so with some passion, some compassion, some humor, and some style." ---Maya Angelou

"Dreams won't work unless you do. Nothing will work unless you do." ---Maya Angelou

"YOU CAN ONLY BECOME TRULY ACCOMPLISHED AT SOMETHING YOU LOVE. DON'T MAKE MONEY YOUR GOAL. INSTEAD PURSUE THE THINGS YOU LOVE DOING AND THEN DO THEM SO WELL THAT PEOPLE CAN'T TAKE THEIR EYES OFF OF YOU." ---Maya Angelou

<u>INTRODUCTION</u>

Romans 8:28, *"And we know that in all things God works for the good of those who love him, who have been called according to his purpose."*

Purpose is a process. We discover, are prepared for, and carry out our purpose through a process. We discover our purpose by going a process of revelation. We are prepared for our purpose by going through a process of preparation. And we fulfill our purpose by process and action over the course of life.

God uses everything in our lives to prepare us to fulfill our divine purpose and destiny. There is no failure in God. Either we are successful or we learn something that makes us stronger and better. Whatever you are going through, just know that God is preparing you, for what is prepared for you. You are growing through, not just going through something.

Purpose is not accomplished over night, but over a life time. "You can't lead where you won't go, (or have never been), and you can't teach what you don't know. Often times we are growing through something that will prepare us to minister to someone else. Jesus had to go through a process to save and serve others. We must go through a process of preparation, before application.

This book is about the process of purpose. There is a process involved in purpose. There is Pain and gain in the process of purpose. Before God uses us, He prepares us to be used. The process of preparation includes a path that goes through valleys, tests and trials that teach, equip, and develop our faith. For without faith, it is impossible to please God and fulfill our divine purpose. The stress, strain, and struggle of our lives, also make us stronger and able to live a life of purpose, and on purpose. **Live on purpose!**

Purpose vs. Process (Excerpt from Andrea Richards Scott 11- 28, 2012)

The process of life is unavoidable

Everyone experiences adversity, challenges, and trials in their lives at one point or another. These difficult experiences are part of the process of life. The things that we seek to avoid are the very things that carve our character and design our destiny. It is human nature to try to avoid unpleasant circumstances, but these situations define, purify, and strengthen us for our purpose. Silver is purified by fire to remove the dross. We are purified by difficulties. I'm reminded of the old saying, 'what doesn't kill you, will make you stronger.' The process of life dictates that we must have experiences in order to grow. The more experiences, the better equipped we become.

Without process, it is unlikely that we will find purpose.

The experiences that we have are a good clue to what our purpose might be. All the things that we try to avoid or forget might be the very things we need to focus on. Have you had a particular challenge in life? That might be the process that is pointing you to your purpose. Have you overcome something great, endured a hardship, recovered from a trauma? All of these are pointers that may lead the way to your purpose. The process can be likened to tea making. Without hot water, a tea bag has no value.

Likewise, without challenges we would not be fit for our purpose. Like coal over time and under pressure, we emerge as diamonds. So the next time you think that your purpose is taking too long or you wonder why you have to go through another challenCge, remember it's a process. Whatever process you are currently going through; embrace it as preparation for your purpose.

PURPOSE LITERATURE REVIEW

Excerpts from (Summary prepared by Nancy Adler in collaboration with the Psychosocial Working group 1997)

Psychological attention to the constructs of purpose in life and meaning in life has its roots in the philosophical writing of Victor Frankl, and in the work of many psychologists who have attempted to theorize about and define positive psychological functioning (e.g., Maslow, Rogers, Jung, Allport, Erikson, Buhler, Neugarten, and Jahoda; see Ryff, 1989; Zika & Chamberlain, 1992, for work that reviews the philosophical and psychological underpinnings of purpose in life).

From his experiences in a concentration camp during W.W. II, Frankl observed that life has meaning under all conditions, and that it is psychologically damaging when a person's search for meaning is blocked (Frankl, 1959, 1967; in Zika & Chamberlain, 1992). This work inspired research, especially by Crumbaugh and colleagues (Crumbaugh, 1968; Crumbaugh & Maholick, 1964), into the concept of purpose and meaning in life.

In a review of work on the construct, Yalom (1980; in Zika & Chamberlain, 1992) found that a lack of meaning in life was associated with psychopathology, while positive life meaning was associated with strong religious beliefs, membership in groups, dedication to a cause, life values, and clear goals.

Lazarus and DeLongis (1983; in Zika & Chamberlain) suggested that sources of personal meaning influence processes of stress and coping.

Antonovsky's (1979) concept of "sense of coherence" includes a "meaningfulness" dimension and was intended to describe a personality construct that "insulates people against the potential harm of stressors on health" (Zika & Chamberlain, 1992, p. 134).

The meaningfulness dimension of sense of coherence is the one that is emphasized the most, and it is intended to capture the extent to which the demands of life are seen as challenges that are worthy of investment and engagement (Seeman, 1991).

Most recently, Ryff (1989; Ryff & Keyes, 1995) has proposed and tested a theoretical model of psychological well-being that includes 6 dimensions of wellness, one of which is purpose in life.

She suggested that a critical component of mental health includes "beliefs that give one the feeling that there is purpose in and meaning to life" (Ryff, 1989, P. 1071). Theories of adult development and maturity include the concept of purpose in life as well:

The definition of maturity ... emphasizes a clear comprehension of life's purpose, a sense of directedness, and intentionality. The lifespan developmental theories refer to a variety of changing purposes or goals in life ... Thus, one functions positively has goals, intentions, and a sense of direction, all of which contribute to the feeling that life is meaningful (Ryff, 1989, p. 1071).

Relationship to Health

Meaningfulness or purpose in life has been related both to physical and psychological health, though the research is not extensive. Petrie and Azariah (1990, in Zika & Chamberlain), using Antonovsky's (1979) "sense of coherence" construct that is made up of three factors (comprehensibility, manageability, and meaningfulness), found that the meaningfulness factor predicted self-reports of pain at a six-month follow-up of a pain-management program. Kass and colleagues (1991) demonstrated that the life purpose scale of their Inventory of Positive Psychological Attitudes scale was negatively correlated with reports of pain and with negative psychological symptoms.

Health behaviors. While they predicted a positive relationship, Spence and Holliman (1995) found no significant association between purpose in life (assessed with Crumbaugb's Purpose in Life test) and African American adolescents' use of prenatal care services. In a study of exposure to violence and victimization among African American adolescents who lived in public housing, DuRant and colleagues (1995) found that purpose in life (assessed with Crumbaugh's Purpose in Life test) was related to the adolescents' number of sexual partners in the last three months.

Psychological health. A number of different studies argue for the mediating effects of meaning in life on well-being. Chamberlain & Zika (1988) found that meaning in life mediated the relationship between religiosity and well-being; Newcomb and Harlow (1986) found that meaninglessness in life (assessed by their meaninglessness measure described above) mediated the relationship between uncontrollable stress and substance use; Harlow, Newcomb, and Bentler (1986) found that meaninglessness mediated between depression and self-derogation.

In two different studies, Zika and Chamberlain (1987, 1992) found strong relationships between meaning in life and a number of different measures of psychological well-being (both positive and negative measures). In their 1987 study of the relation of hassles and personality to subjective well-being, Zika and Chamberlain found that meaning in life (measured by Crumbaugh's Purpose in Life test) had consistent and direct effects on reports of well-being.

THE PATH OF PURPOSE

*4 Yea, though I walk through the valley of the shadow of death,
I will fear no evil; For You are with me; Your rod and Your staff,
they comfort me. 5 You prepare a table before me in the presence of
my enemies…* --- Psalm 23:4-5 (NKJV)

The path of purpose goes through a valley of the shadow of death. Before you get to the prepared table, we must go through the valley. And before we get to our prepared table, we must go through a valley.

Note that the valley of the shadow of death, is on the path to purpose. You can be in the will of God and in a valley of testing. The valley is designed by God to develop our faith in the Shepherd. God grows us through valleys and storms.

This is a part of our purpose "Boot Camp" preparation. God puts us on a path of preparation that can go through storms and valleys. But the disciples going through the storm, also had Jesus on board the ship. And He can say "Peace, Be Still", when we call on him. We can also have faith in his words "Let us go over to the other side". Even in the midst of the storms on the path of purpose, we have the presence and word of God.

Even in the valley on the path of purpose. We can fear no evil, for God is with us, and the rod and staff of God comforts us along the way. There will be peace in the valley on the path of purpose.

So if you are going through a valley or a storm, don't give up. It is a part of the process of your path to your purpose. All things work together to accomplish our divine purpose. God does not waste any experiences. Manure is fertilizer.

Are you going through some s**t, or are you being fertilized for your purpose? The good, bad, ugly, and the stinky, are on the path to purpose.

Now it came to pass on a certain day, that he went into a ship with his disciples: and he said unto them, Let us go over unto the other side of the lake. ......24 And they came to him, and awoke him, saying, Master, master, we perish. Then he arose, and rebuked the wind and the raging of the water: and they ceased, and there was a calm. 25 And he said unto them, Where is your faith? And they being afraid wondered, saying one to another, What manner of man is this! for he commandeth even the winds and water, and they obey him. (Luke 8: 22-25)

The path of purpose can also include storms on the way to the "other side" of your purpose. Jesus said to his disciples "let us go over", not let us go under. But they like we must learn what manner of man we serve.

If God brought you to it, God will take you through it. But the storm fertilizes our faith. And when we run from the storms of purpose, we will run into another storm, or we run with the storm. We must learn to stand still, and let the storm pass. It did not come to stay, it came to pass beloved. And when we feel overwhelmed, we can call on the one that the winds and sea obey.

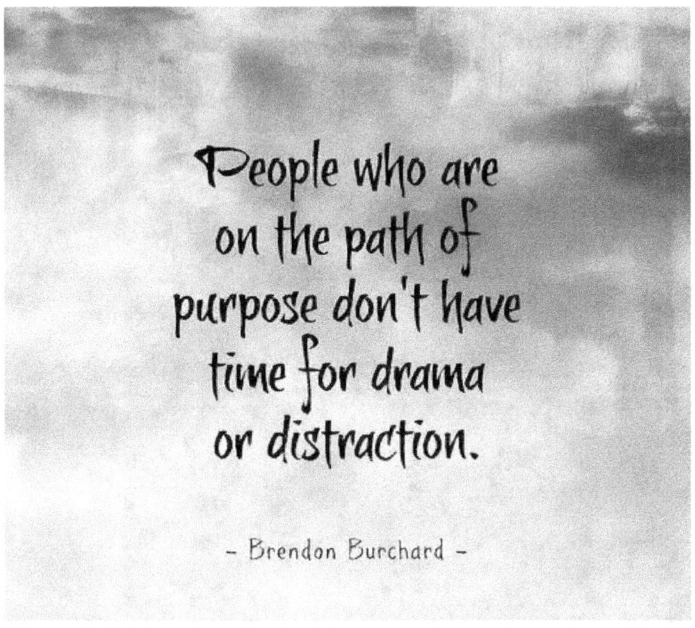

I truly believe that everything that we do and everyone that we meet is put in our path for a purpose. There are no accidents; we're all teachers - if we're willing to pay attention to the lessons we learn, trust our positive instincts and not be afraid to take risks or wait for some miracle to come knocking at our door. -- Marla Gibbs

You didn't accidentally get your personality, looks and gifts. You were designed on purpose to be the way you are. You have what you need to fulfill your destiny. I've learned nothing happens by accident. God knows what He is doing. Every valley has a blessing, and every valley has a purpose. There's no use getting upset and letting trials sour your life. God promises His people victory! One day, you will look back and see what He was up to. You'll say like I did, "Lord, thank you for preparing me in the valley!" -Joel Osteen

THE PAIN OF PURPOSE (No Pain, No Purpose Gain)

There is purpose in pain. Dr. Paul Brand, a great medical missionary, worked with lepers and saw the suffering that they went through. One of the problems with leprosy is that the leper can no longer feel pain in the leprous parts of his body, and Dr. Brand talked about what a tragedy that was. He said, "If I had the power to eliminate human pain, I would not exercise that right. Pain's value is too great."

There is a protecting purpose of pain. Dr. Brand said that when a healthy person has an injured leg, he develops a limp that causes him not to put weight down on it. A leper will sometimes wear away a wounded part of his body because he feels no pain. He might burn a cigarette down until it burns his skin and never feel it. He doesn't have pain to protect him. Pain tells us something is wrong and protects us from harm.

Pain is also a part of the "perfecting process"

To perfect the rose, you must prune the rose. Pruning involves cutting and removing parts of the rose to enable it to grow better. There may be branches that are not producing so it is cut off.

Sometimes God removes people, or things from our lives that may be hindering our ultimate growth and development. Pruning is painful to the rose, and to people, when God prunes us to improve us. Pruning is painful but can lead to perfection. God prunes us, to improve us.

The devil has to get permission to put pain on us

(Job 1: 8-12) *Then the LORD said to Satan, "Have you considered my servant Job? There is no one on earth like him; he is blameless and upright, a man who fears God and shuns evil."*

[9] "Does Job fear God for nothing?" Satan replied. [10] "Have you not put a hedge around him and his household and everything he has? You have blessed the work of his hands, so that his flocks and herds are spread throughout the land. [11] But now stretch out your hand and strike everything he has, and he will surely curse you to your face."

[12] The LORD said to Satan, "Very well, then, everything he has is in your power, but on the man himself do not lay a finger." Then Satan went out from the presence of the LORD.

Please not that Satan has to get permission to put pain on Job. And God put restrictions on Satan as to what he could and could not do to Job. Satan has to get permission before he messes with the person in the process of purpose.

God allowed Satan to put some serious pain on Job. But job was faithful, even though he had his moments. We can have our moments also, and in the end still decide to trust God, though we feel slayed in the moment. We like Job can trust God, even when we can't trace God, or figure God out. Job stated Job 13:15 states, *"Though he slay me, yet will I trust in him"*.

(John 16:22). *"Therefore you now have sorrow; but I will see you again and your heart will rejoice, and your joy no one will take from you"*.

The beauty of a single pearl, or a string of the precious stones, is unmistakable. Few Jewels capture the eye quite like a perfect pearl. Know how the pearl came to be? In the beginning, it's only a grain of sand. That tiny little irritant slips inside the tight seal of an oyster's shell, and immediately causes discomfort. With no way to expel the grain of sand, with no way to ease the pain, the oyster coats the sand with a layer of the inner lining of its shell to make the sand smooth. This still does not ease the oyster's suffering.

Again and again the oyster coats the sand, but all the attempts to get rid of the irritant have little effect. As far as an oyster is concerned, what we call a "pearl" is nothing more than great suffering. But one day the oyster is fished from the water and opened. The gem inside has amazing beauty and holds great value – all because the oyster had great pain and suffering. No pain, no purpose gain!

We must embrace pain and burn it as fuel for our journey. --Kenji Miyazawa

You gain strength, courage, and confidence by every experience in which you really stop to look fear in the face. You are able to say to yourself, 'I lived through this horror. I can take the next thing that comes along. --Eleanor Roosevelt

James 1:2-4 *[2]Consider it pure joy, my brothers and sisters, whenever you face trials of many kinds, [3]because you know that the testing of your faith produces perseverance. [4]Let perseverance finish its work so that you may be mature and complete, not lacking anything.*

So count it all joy, all that you're going through
Even when you're feeling down
Count it all joy, each moment's a gift to you
So turn it all around
And even in the darkest night
If you look hard enough
There's a trace of sunlight waiting there
Yes waiting there for you ("Count it all joy!" The Winans)

On Pain
Kahlil Gibran

Your pain is the breaking of the shell that encloses your understanding.
Even as the stone of the fruit must break, that its heart may stand in the sun, so must you know pain.
And could you keep your heart in wonder at the daily miracles of your life, your pain would not seem less wondrous than your joy;
And you would accept the seasons of your heart, even as you have always accepted the seasons that pass over your fields.
And you would watch with serenity through the winters of your grief.

Much of your pain is self-chosen.
It is the bitter potion by which the physician within you heals your sick self.
Therefore trust the physician, and drink his remedy in silence and tranquility:
For his hand, though heavy and hard, is guided by the tender hand of the Unseen,
And the cup he brings, though it burn your lips, has been fashioned of the clay which the Potter has moistened with His own sacred tears.

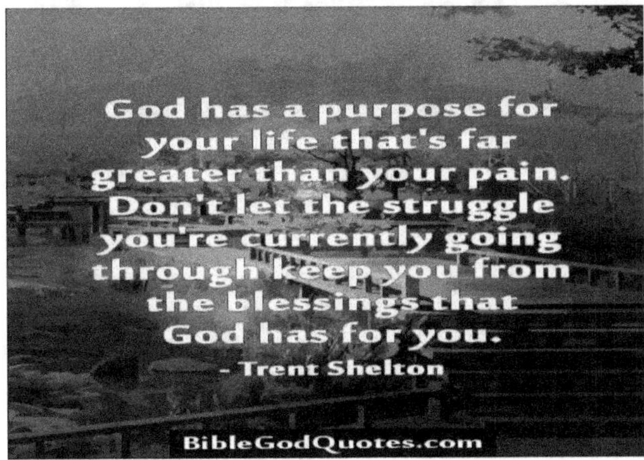

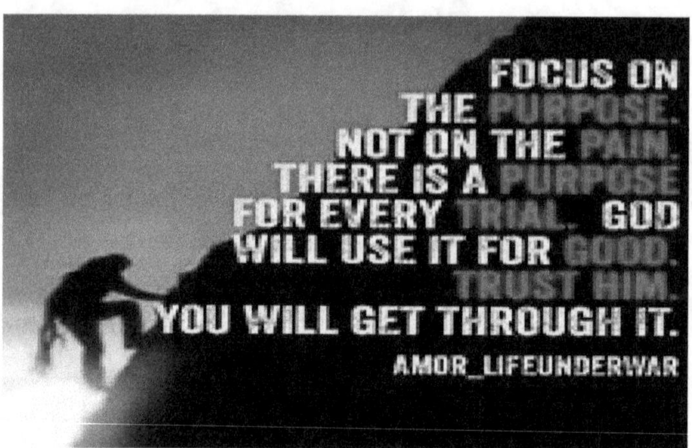

VISION GIVES PAIN A PURPOSE.
PEOPLE WITHOUT VISION
WANDER AIMLESSLY DOWN
THE PATH WITH THE LEAST PAIN.
ON THE CONTRARY,
PEOPLE WITH VISION ARE ABLE
TO ENDURE THE PAIN BECAUSE THEY CAN SEE
THE REWARD LYING AHEAD,
AND THEY KNOW IT WILL
BE WORTH THEIR SACRIFICE.

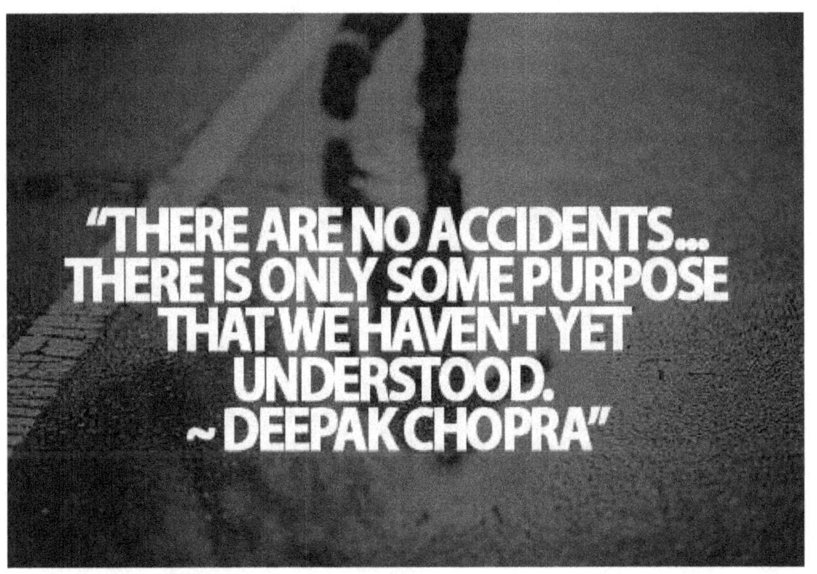

"THERE ARE NO ACCIDENTS...
THERE IS ONLY SOME PURPOSE
THAT WE HAVEN'T YET
UNDERSTOOD.
~ DEEPAK CHOPRA"

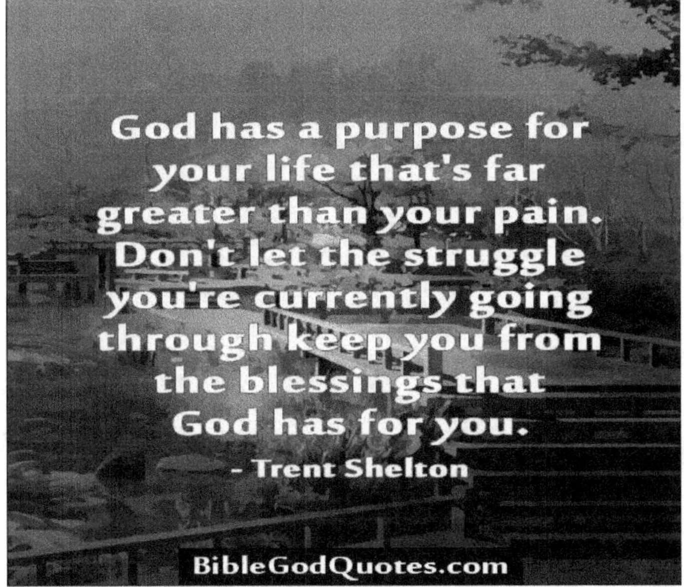

God has a purpose for
your life that's far
greater than your pain.
Don't let the struggle
you're currently going
through keep you from
the blessings that
God has for you.
- Trent Shelton
BibleGodQuotes.com

THE PATIENCE OF PURPOSE

For ye have need of patience, that, after ye have done the will of God, ye might receive the promise. Hebrews 10:36

Because purpose is a process, patience is required to go through the process. Purpose is not accomplished in a day, but over a life time. Understanding delayed gratification is a good way to conceptualize patience and purpose. **Delayed gratification**, or deferred **gratification**, is the ability to resist the temptation for an immediate reward and wait for a later reward. Generally, **delayed gratification** is associated with resisting a smaller but more immediate reward in order to receive a larger or more enduring reward later.

The marshmallow experiment is a famous test of this concept conducted by Walter Mischel at Stanford University and discussed by Daniel Goleman in his popular work. In the 1960s, a group of four-year olds were given a marshmallow and promised another, only if they could wait 20 minutes before eating the first one. Some children could wait and others could not. The researchers then followed the progress of each child into adolescence, and demonstrated that those with the ability to wait were better adjusted and more dependable (determined via surveys of their parents and teachers), and scored an average of 210 points higher on the Scholastic Aptitude Test.

Delay is not denial of purpose. Delay can be the preparation of purpose. Delay is a part of the development of purpose. Delay can also be the maintenance of purpose. When flying it is not uncommon to have maintenance delays. The pilot will speak to the passengers and ask for patience during the temporary delay. The plane needs routine and sometimes emergency maintenance. In both cases the plane is delayed for a while. The delay is not to deny the plane, but to fix the plane and make it better. The delays in our lives are not a denial of our purpose, but a time of maintenance for our purpose.

Sometimes the pilot of the plane puts it in a holding pattern. Holding patterns allow the landing destination to be prepared for landing. Sometimes other planes are in the way, and the holding pattern allows the time needed to make room for landing on the ground.

Sometimes God puts us in a holding pattern in our lives and we can feel stuck. But often God is getting you ready, and or, getting your purpose landing place ready. Either way, delay is not denial, but a part of the process, and patience is required.

Jon Mertz in a post on ThinDifference.com, explores the relationship between purpose and patience. He states:

"As we look at our own initiatives, we get anxious. We try shortcuts or get started and never finish. There are no shortcuts to leading on purpose. And not finishing your purpose is a true waste of valuable time.

Patience really means taking time to do the work. Risk is present in patience yet a patient presence mitigates risk. Our focus needs to be on purpose first and then patiently doing the work to achieve our purpose.

Millennials leaders have been characterized in many different ways, including impatient and filled with purpose. Having a sense of urgency in having an impact is a good thing. Nervous energy can distract us though. Doing the work necessary to have a long-lasting impact combines the best of patience and purpose."

Mertz continues:

My challenge and experience to share with Millennial leaders are to remember:

- *Purpose is to act upon what our talents, passions, soul, and mind are whispering for us to do. Listen closely. Act accordingly.*
- *Patience is how we do the work necessary to realize our purpose. Use your patience to enhance your talents. Use your patience to collaborate and move your purpose forward each and every day.*

(The Role of Patience in Purpose by Jon Mertz January 14, 2015 Thin Difference.com)

Patience is a grounding force in our lives. Patience reminds us that even if we are infinitely powerful and creative, we are not in control of absolutely everything. Sometimes we have to work for our goals and manifest our dreams, while letting go of the deadlines. We can learn to surrender, and trust that things will happen without trying to force them to arrive at the pace we dictate. This can be a humbling yet potentially liberating lesson.

Our mind wants the world to move as fast as we do - as soon as we desire something, our mind wants it - right here, right now. Patience teaches us to slow down. It helps us not to get caught up in the immediacy of the demands of our mind, and, instead, to take a step back and just observe them. Maybe we find that we still want the thing and the time waiting just sharpens our appreciation of it, or maybe we find that the desire fades, and we recognize that its grip on us was just an illusion.

Patience can help us understand that our agenda and timescale is not always the best or right way. It's certainly not the only way. It teaches us to go with the flow and be flexible. If we can do that, we can learn to be happy whatever curve balls life throws our way. (Jade Lizzie @ Yogapedia)

THE PROVISION PROSPERITY AND PAYOFF OF PURPOSE

Is. 58:11 *And the LORD shall guide thee continually, and satisfy thy soul in drought, and make fat thy bones: and thou shalt be like a watered garden, and like a spring of water, whose waters fail not.*

There is synergy between purpose and prosperity. --Matt Hudson

"We can have more than we've got because we can become more than we are." – Jim Rohn

Purpose + Passion + Process = Payoff

When you find purpose in what you do, exhibit passion for the outcome, and master the process to make it happen, you produce the payoffs you want, need, and deserve.

If God brought you to it, He will take you through it! He would not bring you this far, and leave you! God will make provision for everything He commissions us to do. Where He leads, He feeds. Where He guides, He provides. God's promised prosperity is for the life lived in union with His eternal purposes

When God sends you somewhere, when He enlists you for a mission, when He leads you to a cause or a ministry, when He takes you by the hand and says "follow me," you can take it to the bank that He will supply your every need.

Psalm 16:7 *I will bless the LORD who guides me; even at night my heart instructs me.*

God will pay, when you obey!

The Bible says, *"… Obey… Then you will be prosperous and successful."* (Joshua 1:8, GN)

Abraham was told to pack up his family and move to a faraway land he had never been to. Noah was told to build an ark when there was no water in sight. Esther was told to go and see the king when she was not summoned which meant almost certain death.

Each of these situations was unsettling at best to the person who was told to do them. The one leading them was God. They each have a common thread – God provided what they needed to do what He asked. Where there is divine purpose, there is divine provision. A person driven by divine purpose, will also be provided by divine purpose.

Where God guides He provides. Learning to trust in the faithfulness of God makes life so much easier. We must train our spirits to see past the physical realm and see the provisional moves of God working favorably on our behalf.

Think about your life. Is God providing you with the necessary "tools" to go in the direction you are taking? Or is God not providing? Remember, only where God guides, will God provide. Where God does not provide, He is not guiding.

Where God leads,
He meets needs.
Where God guides,
he provides.

God didn't
promise days
without pain,
laughter without
sorrow, or sun
without rain,
but
He did promise
strength for the
day, comfort for
the tears, and
light for the
way.
If God brings
you to it, He will
bring you
through it.
Fb/HugsandKissess

If God brings you to it,
He will bring you through it.
In Happy moments, praise God.
In Difficult moments, seek God.
In Quiet moments, worship God.
In Painful moments, trust God.
In Every moment, thank God.
PRAISE-ALLAH.TUMBLR.COM

THE PASSION OF PURPOSE

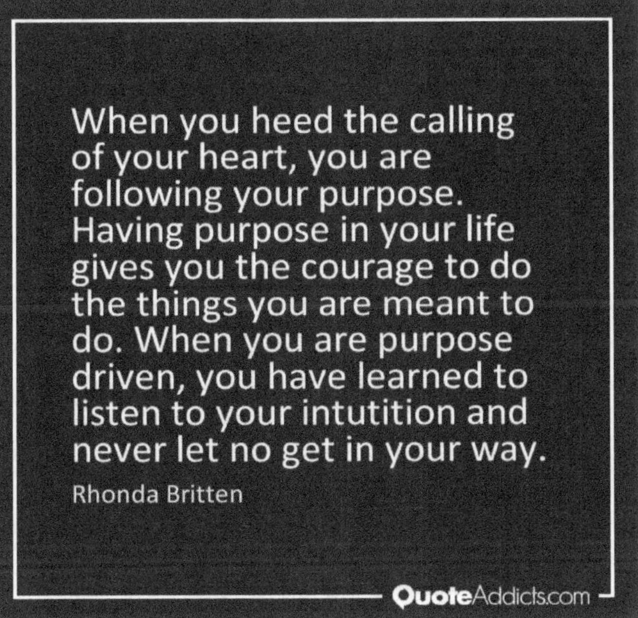

Allow your passion to become your purpose, and it will one day become your profession.

"Persistence. Perfection. Patience. Power. Prioritize your passion. It keeps you sane." — Criss Jami, Killosophy

My general formula for my students is "Follow your bliss." Find where it is, and don't be afraid to follow it. -- Joseph Campbell

"Choose your love, and love your choice." — Thomas S. Monson

Make doing the things that make you feel good a priority. Prioritize your bliss. Bliss is that deep, fulfilling, sustainable, driving need you have. That thing that is the true 'you'. Your bliss is your life's purpose. It is what makes you feel most fulfilled. Your bliss gives your otherwise meaningless life meaning. Your bliss leads to a satisfied self-actualized life.

Your bliss and passion is a clue to what your purpose is. The creator pre-wired us to enjoy what we were meant to do. Our purpose is a function of our passion and bliss. If you want to know your purpose, search your passions and bliss. And then follow it, and fulfill your purpose. Prioritize your happiness and bliss. You are responsible for your bliss, so you must make it a priority.

Who else is going to make my bliss important other than me? We show others how to treat us by how they see us treating ourselves. If others see you neglect yourself and put your own happiness last, they may think its ok for them to neglect you too. Love others as you love yourself. Prioritize your bliss and happiness and make it most important. Your bliss is your most important priority. Make it so!

"All the time. It is miraculous. I even have a superstition that has grown on me as a result of invisible hands coming all the time - namely, that if you do follow your bliss you put yourself on a kind of track that has been there all the while, waiting for you, and the life that you ought to be living is the one you are living. When you can see that, you begin to meet people who are in your field of bliss, and they open doors to you. I say, follow your bliss and don't be afraid, and doors will open where you didn't know they were going to be." (Joseph Campbell)

Explore the Things You Love To Do & What Comes Easy to You

We are all born with a deep and meaningful purpose that we have to discover. Your purpose is not something you need to makeup; it's already there. You have to uncover it in order to **create the life you want**. You can begin to discover your purpose by exploring two things:

1. What do you love to do?
2. What comes easily to you?

Align Your Goals with Your Life Purpose and Passions

We're all gifted with a set of talents and interests that tell us what we're supposed to be doing. Once you know what your life purpose is, organize all of your activities around it. Everything you do should be an expression of your purpose. If an activity or goal doesn't fit that formula, don't work on it.

Aligning with your purpose is most critical when setting professional goals. When it comes to personal goals, you have more flexibility. If you want to learn how to paint or water ski, go ahead and do so. If your goal is to get fit and lose weight, move ahead with confidence. Nurturing yourself emotionally, physically and spiritually will make you more energized, resilient and motivated to live your purpose on the professional front.

However, don't ignore the signs that your job or career is not right for you. If you dread Monday mornings and live for the weekends, it may be a sign that it's time to follow your heart and pursue the work you long to do. (Jack canfield blog.)

Allow your passion to become your purpose, and it will one day become your profession.

Quoteistan.com

If you can't figure out your purpose, figure out your *passion*. For your passion will *lead* you right into your *purpose*

Bishop T.D. Jakes

THE PRODUCE OF PURPOSE: GOALS

Purpose to set goals

"A person who aims at nothing is sure to hit it." – Anonymous

"People who consistently win have a clear and thoughtful strategy. They know what they need to do and when they need to do it. They write it down so they stay on course, and avoid any alternative that does not get them closer to the finish line." — Dr.Phil

"When a man does not know what harbor he is making for, no wind is the right wind." Seneca

"Having a purpose is the difference between making a living and making a life." Tom Thiss

"Efforts and courage are not enough without purpose and direction." John F. Kennedy

"True happiness… is not attained through self-gratification, but through fidelity to a worthy purpose." Helen Keller

"The trouble with not having a goal is that you can spend your life running up and down the field and never score" – Bill Copeland

The produce of purpose are tangible goals. When we are driven by purpose, we set and accomplish real tangible goals to fulfill that purpose. There is joy in setting and accomplishing goals. Accomplishing goals that you set for yourself feed your self-esteem. Your sense of self efficacy. It gives you self-confidence. That can't be taken away because it is within you. Decide to set goals. Identify your desires. Set goals based on your desired outcomes. Compose a plan to accomplish them. Execute your plan.

A goal gives one a since of direction. Without a goal, we can't tell if we are going in the wrong direction. Without a goal there is no wrong direction. A map is not much good if there is no goal or destination. Goals give us something to aim for. Sin is defined as missing the mark. Not having a mark is worse than sin. Those who have life goals early in life, are far more successful, and waste less of their time than those who have not set goals for themselves.

"Definiteness of Purpose with a Burning Desire to achieve it, followed by Focused Actions until you achieve your goal is the secret to success." – Neo

Steps for reaching your goals:

Write out your goals. Put your goals, reasons, objectives and beliefs in writing. When they are in writing it makes them more real and they can be reviewed and used as a constant source of encouragement. Eventually your goals will become branded in your mind.

Watch for Negative Self Talk. Talk back to negative self-talk with positive affirmations. Never say I can't. Always say I can.

Make a plan for reaching your goals. Your plan becomes your road map and helps you determine the best course to follow. Be willing to change it as you go along.

Minimize Distractions. Get rid of as much temptation as possible that deviates from your focus on your goal. If for example your goal is to exercise more and you have identified watching TV as a distraction, don't turn on the TV until you have achieved the tasks relating to your goal. Use every method you can think of to remove distractions from your life and it will help you maintain focus.

Use the Power of Visualization. To have something to focus on we must have a strong visual picture of our target so we can maintain focus on the end result. The more you bring what it is you wish to obtain to the forefront of your mind, the more focus you can give to it.

Use vision boards with pictures of your desired outcomes. Vision boards are places that you put text and images describing or symbolizing the goals and dreams that you want to create. Making a collage of positive images that represent what you want to have in your life—love, success, travel, and so on—is a great way to stimulate your thoughts and emotions. Put vision boards up in your office, your bedroom, or anywhere else you spend a lot of time. Look at them, think about them, and get excited when you see them. These boards are a great way to practice the law of attraction and to use your positive thoughts and feelings to manifest what you want.

Measure Your Progress. Inspect what you expect. Create a system and timetable to measure your progress. This can tell you if you are on track or if you need to make adjustments to either your plan or activities.

Prioritize your Goal. Focus on one goal at one time. Try not to overburden yourself as it will limit your chance of achieving your goal and demotivate you. Concentrate on the important ones first, achieve them and then you can look at addressing the other goals.

If you try to do a bunch of things at once, nothing will get done. If you wave a magnifying glass around on the hottest day, you won't burn anything. You'll dissipate all your energy among the trivial many. By focusing and harnessing all your power, energy, time, focus, thinking, etc. on one goal, you will be amazed at how quickly you can accomplish it. Just as you steady a magnifying glass on a single object, with the hot burning sun rays analogous to your desire, focus, power, energy, time, etc., you will make accelerated progress.

Work your Goals into your Daily Plan. Do something towards achieving your goal as often as you can. The best way to achieve your goals and maintain your focus is to do something that will make it happen each and every day.

Give your goal daily attention and you'll remain more focused.

Benefits of having goals in life

- Makes you feel more fulfilled
- It creates your daily life with enthusiasm and joy
- It gives you direction and focus
- It helps you understand what is unimportant for you in life and it frees you from things that don't matter
- It helps you to gain your success.

"If you want to be happy, set a goal that commands your thoughts, liberates your energy and inspires your hopes." — Andrew Carnegie

"Our goals can only be reached through a vehicle of a plan, in which we must fervently believe, and upon which we must vigorously act. There is no other route to success." — Pablo Picasso

"Success is the progressive realization of a worthy goal or ideal." — Earl Nightingale

"By recording your dreams and goals on paper, you set in motion the process of becoming the person you most want to be. Put your future in good hands – your own." — Mark Victor Hansen

"The trouble with not having a goal is that you can spend your life running up and down the field and never score." — Bill Copeland

"All successful people have a goal. No one can get anywhere unless he knows where he wants to go and what he wants to be or do. " — Norman Vincent Peale

"A goal properly set is halfway reached." — Zig Ziglar

THE PEACE OF PURPOSE

Thou wilt keep him in perfect peace, whose mind is stayed on thee: because he trusteth in thee. Isaiah 26:3

Philippians 4:6-7 states: *"Be anxious for nothing, but in everything by prayer and supplication, with thanksgiving, let your requests be made known to God; and the peace of God, which surpasses all understanding, will guard your hearts and minds through Christ Jesus."*

Purpose produces peace and contentment of mind. There is a peace in knowing you are living and doing your divine purpose. There is peace in knowing you are doing what you were meant to do. Working in your purpose may be sometime difficult, but there is satisfaction in knowing I am doing what I am supposed to be doing.

A lack of peace of mind will result in doing things that are off purpose. When we are doing things that are off purpose, there can be no contentment of mind. When we are doing that which we know is the will of God for us, we experience the peace of God. The peace of God is found in doing the will of God. There can only be frustration when one knows they are not doing what God wants them to do.

Jonah in the Bible ran from his purpose and ran into a storm. God had plans for Jonah, 'but Jonah ran …' (Jonah 1:3). Often this is the case with us.

But Jonah ran away from the LORD and headed for Tarshish. He went down to Joppa, where he found a ship bound for that port. After paying the fare, he went aboard and sailed for Tarshish to flee from the LORD. (Jonah 1:3)

Jonah ran away from God and went "down" to Joppa. Whenever we run from the will of God, we go down. Our spirit is down. Our mind is down and we have little peace of mind. There can be no peace of mind when I know I am out of the will of god. When we run from the will of God, we go down like Jonah. When we know we are in the will of God, there is peace and contentment of mind. We also have the comfort of the Holy Spirit to aid us in doing the will of God.

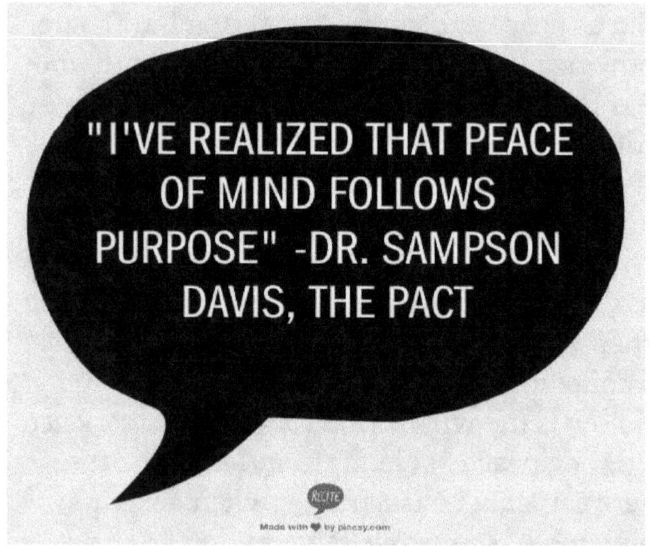

"Peace is not merely a distant goal we seek but a means by which we arrive at that goal." ~Martin Luther King Jr.

"Until you make peace with who you are, you will never be content with what you have." ~Doris Mortman

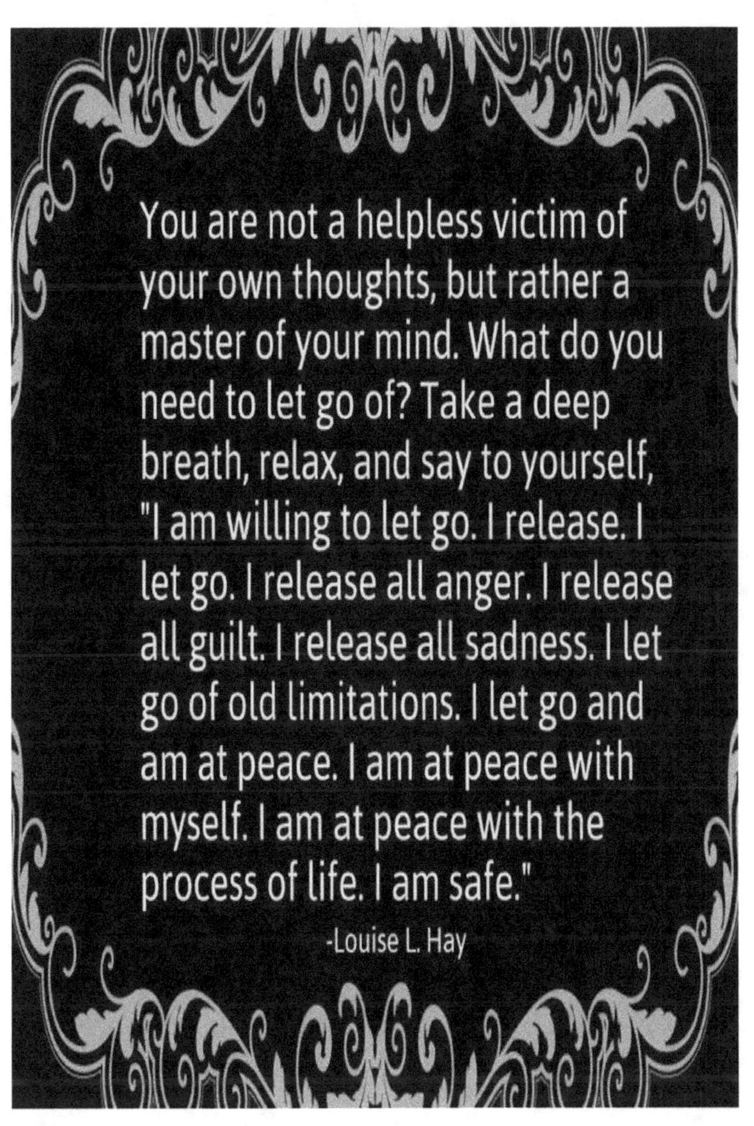
You are not a helpless victim of your own thoughts, but rather a master of your mind. What do you need to let go of? Take a deep breath, relax, and say to yourself, "I am willing to let go. I release. I let go. I release all anger. I release all guilt. I release all sadness. I let go of old limitations. I let go and am at peace. I am at peace with myself. I am at peace with the process of life. I am safe."
-Louise L. Hay

THE PEOPLE OF PURPOSE
(Serving)

Helping and serving others with our talents and gifts, is the solution for vain living.

"Our prime purpose in this life is to help others. And if you can't help them, at least don't hurt them." --Dalai Lama

"The purpose of human life is to serve, and to show compassion and the will to help others." --Albert Schweitzer

"To ease another's heartache is to forget one's own." — Abraham Lincoln

"I am because we are, and because we are, I am." — African Proverb

Strong social support correlates with an astonishing number of desirable outcomes. For instance, research by Julianne Holt-Lunstad, Timothy Smith, and Bradley Layton shows that high levels of social support predict longevity as reliably as regular exercise does, and low social support is as damaging as high blood pressure.

The benefits of social support are not just physical. In a study of 1,648 students at Harvard that Shawn Achor conducted with Phil Stone and Tal Ben-Shahar, they found that social support was the greatest predictor of happiness during periods of high stress.

That study focused on how much social support the students received. But in follow-on research Achor conducted in March 2011, he found that even more important to sustained happiness and engagement was the amount of social support the students provided.

For example, how often does a student help others when they are overwhelmed with work? How often does he initiate social interactions on the job? Social support providers — people who picked up slack for others, invited coworkers to lunch, and organized office activities — were not only 10 times more likely to be engaged at work than those who kept to themselves; they were 40% more likely to get a promotion.

Some studies suggest that we can move our happiness set point permanently higher by helping others. According to one such study that analyzed data from the German Socio-Economic Panel Survey, a collection of statistics representing the largest and longest-standing series of observations on happiness in the world, the trait most strongly associated with long-term increases in life satisfaction is, in fact, a persistent commitment to pursuing altruistic goals. That is, the more we focus on compassionate action, on helping others, the happier we seem to become in the long run.

According to another study, altruism doesn't just correlate with an increase in happiness; it actually *causes* it — at least in the short term. When psychologist Sonja Lyubomirsky had students perform five acts of kindness of their choosing per week over the course of six weeks, they reported a significant increase in their levels of happiness relative to a control group of students who didn't.

According to Dr. David R. Hamilton, acts of kindness create an emotional warmth, which releases a hormone known as oxytocin. Oxytocin causes the release of a chemical called nitric oxide, which dilates the blood vessels. This reduces blood pressure and, therefore, oxytocin is known as a "cardio-protective" hormone. It protects the heart by lowering blood pressure.

Choose to be kind and do kind acts for others. You can benefit your heart, reduce anxiety, lower blood pressure, and simply be a happier human being.

In another study, published in 2010 in the *Journal of Social Psychology*, researchers in Great Britain had participants take a survey measuring life satisfaction, then they assigned all 86 participants to one of three groups. One group was instructed to perform a daily act of kindness for the next 10 days. Another group was also told to do something new each day over those 10 days. A third group received no instructions. After the 10 days were up, the researchers asked the participants to complete the life satisfaction survey again.

The groups that practiced kindness and engaged in novel acts both experienced a significant—and roughly equal—boost in happiness; the third group didn't get any happier. The findings suggest that good deeds do in fact make people feel good—even when performed over as little as 10 days—and there may be particular benefits to varying our acts of kindness, as novelty seems linked to happiness as well.

"Kindness in words creates confidence. Kindness in thinking creates profoundness. Kindness in giving creates love."-- Lao Tzu

"We are constituted so that simple acts of kindness, such as giving to charity or expressing gratitude, have a positive effect on our long-term moods. The key to the happy life, it seems, is the good life: a life with sustained relationships, challenging work, and connections to community." --Paul Bloom

If I can Help Somebody

If I can help somebody
As I travel along
If I can help somebody
With a word or song
If I can help somebody
From doing wrong
My living shall not be in vain.

Chorus:
My living shall not be in vain
My living shall not be in vain
If I can help somebody
While I'm singing this song
My living shall not be in vain.

If I can do my duty
As a good man ought
If I can bring back beauty
To a world up wrought
If I can spread love's message
As the Master taught
Then my living shall not be in vain.

Chorus:
My living shall not be in vain
My living shall not be in vain
If I can help somebody
While I'm singing this song
My living shall not be in vain.

"If I Can Help Somebody" was written by Alma Bazel Androzzo,
and has been performed by Mahalia Jackson.

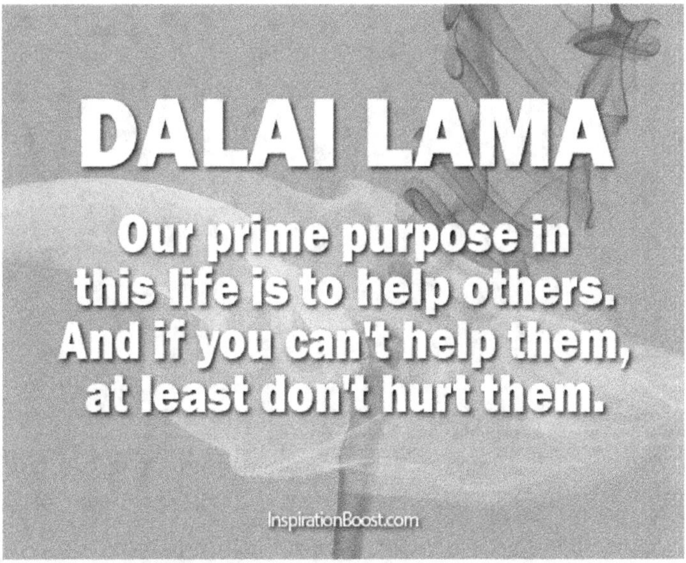

DALAI LAMA
Our prime purpose in
this life is to help others.
And if you can't help them,
at least don't hurt them.
InspirationBoost.com

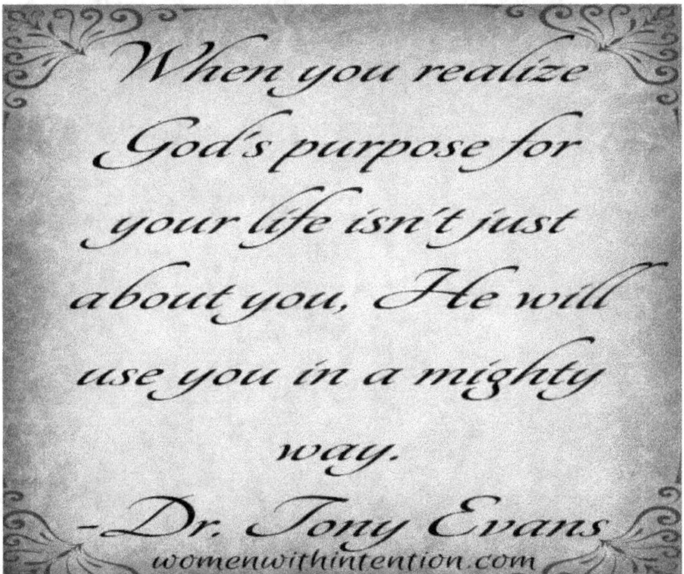

When you realize
God's purpose for
your life isn't just
about you, He will
use you in a mighty
way.
-Dr. Tony Evans
womenwithintention.com

> The purpose of life is to matter, to be productive, to have it make a difference that you lived at all-using the talents that God has given you for the betterment of others.
>
> Leo Rosten

THE PROFIT OF PURPOSE

"For what shall it profit a man, if he shall gain the whole world, and lose his own soul?" – Mark 8:36

Imagine a pill that would reduce cognitive decline (Alzheimer's disease) by 40-50%. Reduce macroscopic stroke by 40%. Aid sleep apnea. And add seven (7) years to your life. Decrease depression and give you a sense of fulfillment. Withstand pain better, have a healthier brain, and immunize you from vain living. Well, that "magic pill" is purpose.

Purpose is most profitable because it feeds and satisfies your soul. Food satisfies the stomach, but what satisfies the soul? *"One thing that is hard to find, is a man or woman with a satisfied mind."* Knowing and being on purpose satisfies the soul and mind.

Mental hunger and frustration will occur when you feel your living is in vain. Being on purpose is the solution for vain living. *"Is my living in vain? No of course not, it's not all in vain. It's eternal gain!"* (Clark Sisters)

Here's what science has to say about the profit of finding and living your purpose. (By: Elise Moreau October 7, 2016 Care2.com)

Having a sense of purpose helps you live longer.
According to one particular study, the physical health benefits of living your purpose is comparable to diet and exercise — it's never too late to start, and the earlier in life that you do start, the earlier the longevity effects of it start to kick in. That's right — finding and living your purpose can increase your lifespan. In examining 14 years' worth of data from over 6,000 subjects, the

researchers found that those who had died reported lower levels of purpose in life while those who reportedly had greater purpose in life had a decreased risk of death regardless of their age.

You may be able to withstand pain better when you have a sense of purpose.

It turns out that by having a sense of purpose, you literally get stronger at dealing with physical pain and discomfort. Research has shown that women who exhibited resilience and a strong sense of purpose in life were more capable of handling pain from heat and cold. This may be similar to the mental and physical strength that athletes are known for. They're able to keep their minds calm and continue to push their bodies close to physical exhaustion — all because they're living what they consider to be their purpose.

A strong sense of purpose might motivate you to value your health more.

If you feel like clean eating and physical exercise is more of a chore than a privilege, maybe you need to get clearer on your life purpose. In a study that was conducted on a group of European teenagers, those who reportedly had a greater sense of purpose were more likely to have healthier diets and regular exercise regimens. And in another related study of over 7,000 Americans, those who reported having greater life purpose were more likely to make better use of preventative healthcare and spent less time in the hospital compared to those with a lower sense of purpose.

You'll have a healthier brain when you have a strong sense of purpose.

Add "find purpose" to the list of things you can do to improve your brain health. Research has suggested that people who have a lower sense of purpose in their lives could be more likely to develop Alzheimer's disease later on in life compared to people who have a greater sense of purpose. People who rated themselves higher on the life purpose scale were found to have a

30-percent reduced risk of cognitive decline compared to people who rated themselves lower on the life purpose scale. (By: Elise Moreau October 7, 2016 Care2.com)

Here are the top seven benefits we each gain by compassionate helping from *THE BLOG* 12/22/2014 "Volunteering – 7 **Big Reasons Why Serving Others Serves Us**" By <u>Kathy Gottberg</u>

1. **More happiness.** According to Stephen G. Post, professor of preventative medicine at Stony Brook University in New York and author of **The Hidden Gifts of Helping**, a part of our brain lights up when we help others. That part of our brain then doles out feel-good chemicals like dopamine, and possibly serotonin. According to Post, "<u>These chemicals help us feel joy and delight – helper's high</u>." A common reaction is that "some people feel more tranquil, peaceful, serene; others, warmer and more trusting." When we volunteer we often give ourselves deeper purpose and meaning and that nearly always leads to greater happiness.

2. **Reduce stress.** When we help others our bodies release a hormone called oxytocin, which buffers stress and helps us maintain social trust and tranquility. Along with oxytocin are the other chemicals like dopamine, which is a mood-elevating neurotransmitter. These drugs tend to push aside negative emotions and <u>reduce the stress level</u>.

3. **Relief from pain.** A <u>study done by Pain Management Nursing</u> reports that on a scale from 0 to 10 that people's pain ratings dropped from nearly 6 to below 4 after attending a volunteer training program and leading discussion groups for fellow sufferers. Volunteering takes our mind off our pain and also makes us feel more in control of it.

4. **Longer lifespan.** Over <u>40 international studies confirm</u> that volunteering can add years to your life. In fact, current studies suggest up to a <u>22% reduction in mortality rates</u>! How much do we have to do? Studies confirm that a regular commitment of as little as 25 hours per year is beneficial.

5. **Lower blood pressure.** A <u>study done by Psychology & Aging</u> reports those adults over 50 who volunteered for 200 hours in the past year were 40 percent less likely to have hypertension than non-volunteers. It is believed this is accomplished because of the lower stress, and the effects of being active, social and altruistic.

6. **Reduce mild depression.** <u>A study of alcoholics going through AA</u> (Alcoholics Anonymous) points out that those who volunteered to help others were twice as likely to stay clean a year later and their depression rates were correspondingly lower as well. Plus, in many cases mild depression is linked to isolation. Volunteering helps to keep a person in regular contact with others and to help develop a social support system.

7. **Benefit your career.** That's right. A book entitled *The Halo Effect* by John Raynolds insists that volunteering for the right reasons can so turn your life around that the benefits will extend to your work. Raynolds says, "Remember, when you become involved, when you lead with your heart as well as your head, the result is always good." Instead of feeling depressed or unfulfilled at work, Raynolds is convinced that you will feel more happy, confident and energized when you find something that makes you feel generous and purposeful — and that of course will spread to every single area of your life.

NOTHING CONTRIBUTES
SO MUCH TO
TRANQUILIZE THE MIND
AS A STEADY
PURPOSE—
A POINT ON WHICH
THE SOUL MAY FIX ITS
INTELLECTUAL EYE.
—MARY SHELLEY

The Push, Pull, & Persistence of Purpose

A person on purpose does what they are supposed to do, when they are supposed to do it, whether they feel like it or not. Purpose driven, not feeling driven. Purpose pushes you pass your feelings. Purpose provides the "Push Factor".

Purpose pushes you pass your comfort zone to fulfillment of your purpose. Purpose makes you get up early, and stay up late. Purpose is what separates folk who succeed, from folk who fail. A sense of purpose will push you pass feelings of quitting. Purpose will give a "made up mind." Purpose will make you get up when you fall and try again and again.

Like a map purpose determines direction. Without a point of location and destination maps are useless. Without a purpose, we could be going anywhere, or nowhere. But purpose determines direction.

Purpose points in the right direction. Without a purpose or destination, there is no wrong way. There is no guide. A life purpose provides guidance and directions for life. Purpose allows us to "Know the time and what must be done! (HEM)." A purpose driven person is never bored.

Purpose pulls. It's what compels you to *do*, to create, to explore and discover. A sense of life purpose promotes physical, mental, and spiritual health. People who seek meaning beyond themselves are healthier, happier, and live longer. It's vital to our well-being that we maintain strong feelings of purpose and community.

THE PERCRIPTION OF PURPOSE
(How to find your purpose)

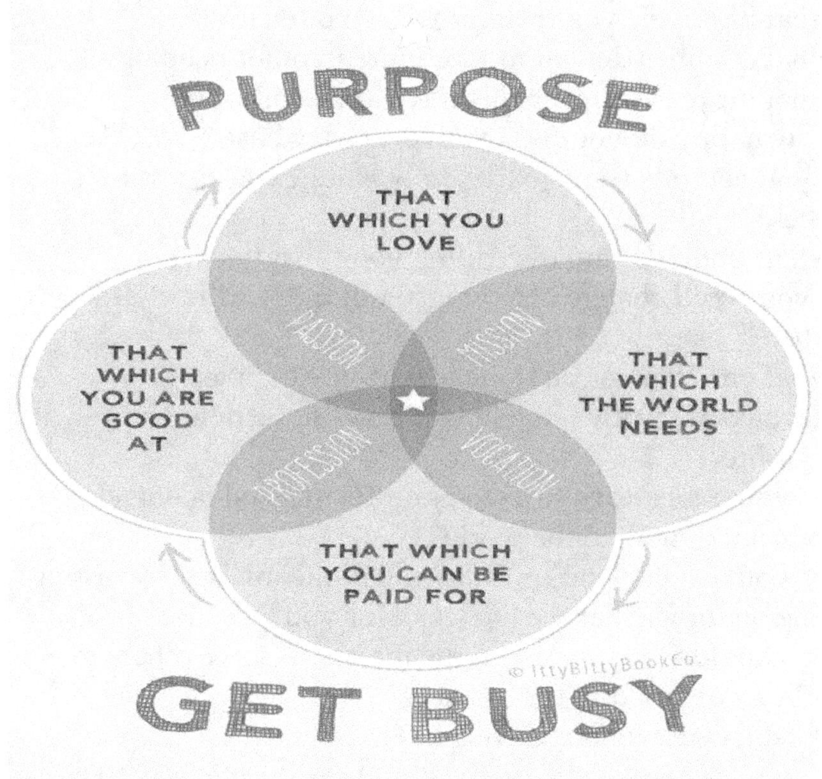

If you don't feel fulfilled by, or happy with your life, you may decide to evaluate your life's purpose. While this can be a challenging self-examination that may lead you to believe that you've been living life the "wrong way," take heart; it's never too late to begin living the life that you want to live — a life that is meaningful and happy. Find your life's purpose, then take action to implement the kind of life you really want to live.

Question yourself. To begin assessing your life's purpose, it's important to assess what you love to do, what you currently do, and what needs to change to live a more purposeful life. Some questions to consider are:

- When have you been happiest in your life?
- What has made you truly proud of yourself?
- What qualities do you most admire in other people?
- What makes you feel really alive and energized?
- How happy do you feel on an everyday basis?
- If you had one week to live, how would you spend that week?
- What "shoulds" are overriding your "want tos"?
- If you could change one thing about the world, what would it be?
- What one change could make your life happier?
- Have you recently felt like you'd like to be doing more with your life?
- Do you often yearn to use your gifts (natural talents) to contribute more to the world?
- Do you feel like you're "majoring in the minors" – wasting time on things that are too small for you?
- Do you desire to "major in the majors" – serve others in a larger way but don't know how?
- Do you ever wonder if "this is it?"
  If you answered "yes" to most of these questions, you're probably ready to unlock the power of purpose.

Purpose determines two things:
- what meaning you derive from your life's experiences
- your ability to make focused and intentional decisions

Okinawans call this **ikigai:** *the reason for which you wake up in the morning.* They live by it and that is why they live long lives. People who retire from work early die early. People who do not have a clear purpose in life have faster rates of mental decline.

So, **purpose is the fuel which gives you direction and helps you to move forward.** It makes your internal spark burn brightly, makes you more productive and helps you to live long.
Finding a purpose for living is the only way to escape a life of mediocrity and meaninglessness.
The dictionary defines purpose as: An object or result aimed at: INTENTION RESOLUTION, DETERMINATION.

What does this suggest? A "purpose" can be as simple as an intention or a resolution. So, a "life purpose" is a choice or intention to live in a certain way. A life purpose is realized through "attention" – by getting to know your authentic self, exploring your gifts or natural talents and passions, and "intention" – choosing the best possible expression to share them with the world.

Finding your purpose is a misleading concept because it's not something we have to go out and "get," but rather something we need to turn within and "unleash." As stated earlier: The word educate means, "to educe out from." To be truly educated, is to have your inner potential educed or brought out. To be self-actualized and have your potential fully realized and manifested.
We've already got it – even if we haven't clearly realized it yet! God had a purpose and calling for our lives before we were born. Our mother's had visions of what we would become even as we were in their wombs. We are born with purpose and on purpose. There are no unforeseen accidents with God. How do we unlock it? By looking in the most obvious places – our gifts, passions, and values, even often our parents who produced us by the grace of God.
Our purpose will always be something that:

- We feel that we are naturally good at and enjoy doing

- We feel passionate and care deeply about
- We feel fits our values and ways we prefer to operate in the world.

Your purpose is what some refer to as a "calling." We all have a calling or purpose for our lives. What is your purpose? What is your "calling"? What problem are you the answer to? What need does you talent or gift meet? Our gift will make room for us in this world, and give us a reason to be. Everyone has a talent or gift that will allow us to make a difference in the world in which we live. Your gift will make room for you.

<u>What have you been called to change, produce, support, help, invent, create, expand, or heal?</u>

Before we can discover our true life purpose, we need to "unlock the clues" that lead to it. Namely, things we love to do, feel passionate about, and are important to our way of being.   The need for purpose is one the defining characteristics of human beings. Human beings crave purpose, and suffer serious psychological difficulties when we don't have it. Purpose is a fundamental component of a fulfilling life.

Richard Leider a bestselling author, keynote speaker, and executive coach states that:

Having a strong sense of purpose can have a powerful positive effect. When you have a sense of purpose, you never get up in the morning wondering what you're going to do with yourself. When you're 'in purpose' - that is, engaged with and working towards your purpose - life becomes easier, less complicated and stressful. You become more mono-focused, like an arrow flying towards its target, and your mind feels somehow taut and strong, with less space for negativity to seep in.

A *powerful example of this comes from Victor Frankl's famous book, Man's Search for Meaning, in which he describes his experiences in <u>concentration</u> camps during the Second World War. Frankl observed that the inmates who were most likely to survival were those who felt they had a goal or purpose. Frankl himself spend a lot of time trying to reconstruct a manuscript he had lost on his journey to the camp - his life's work. Others held on to a vision of their future - seeing their loved ones again or a major task to complete once they were free.*

"There is no greater gift you can give or receive than to honor your calling. It's why you were born. And how you become most truly alive."

☙ OPRAH WINFREY

Find Your Calling: 5 Steps to Identify Your Purpose *By* Amy Kessel

The Bible is very clear as to what our purpose in life should be. Men in both the Old and New Testaments sought for and discovered life's purpose. Solomon, the wisest man who ever lived, discovered the futility of life when it is lived only for this world. He gives these concluding remarks in the book of Ecclesiastes: "Here is the conclusion of the matter: Fear God and keep his commandments, for this is the whole duty of man. For God will bring every deed into judgment, including every hidden thing, whether it is good or evil" (Ecclesiastes 12:13-14).

1. Notice what captivates you.
Check out your bedside reading table, your Amazon wish list, and the collection of blogs you follow. What most excites you, or enrages you? What would you like to write an op-ed about? Why?

2. Take your life inventory, reflecting past callings.
Acknowledge what you learned from acting on older callings, and see if anything from those experiences remains alive for you. Retrieve bits that might help you in deciphering your current calling. Put your old callings to rest if they are no longer alive for you, so you can open space for new callings to arise.

3. Journal on what your calling is.
Write out 50 responses to the question: "What is my calling?" Put pen to paper and go! Do not pause or edit, and do not stop before you get to 50. Your calling *will* make itself known. It will probably also make you cry. This is good news.
(Note: Steve Pavlina wrote a wonderful post that elaborates on this idea: How to Discover Your Life Purpose in About 20 Minutes.)

4. Ask others what they think.

Poll your friends and family about your passions. Ask them what they see as your calling. Notice which responses elicit a feeling of "yes!" in you.

5. Use your values as a guide.

Make a list of your core values (these are qualities that make you, you; they aren't who you think you should be, but rather who you already are). How are you honoring those values in your life right now? What information do your values give you about your calling?

Living our lives by honoring our callings creates deep contentment and, by extension, a more vibrant world. What's whispering in your ear? What will you do about it?

(Amy Kessel is a Certified Life Coach who helps women create healthy change in their personal and professional lives. Her free eCourse, "Reclaiming Your Brilliance", provides women with inspiration to jumpstart the change process.)

> WORK FOR A CAUSE,
> NOT FOR APPLAUSE.
> LIVE LIFE TO EXPRESS,
> NOT TO IMPRESS.
> DON'T STRIVE TO
> MAKE YOUR
> PRESENCE NOTICED,
> JUST MAKE YOUR
> ABSENCE FELT.

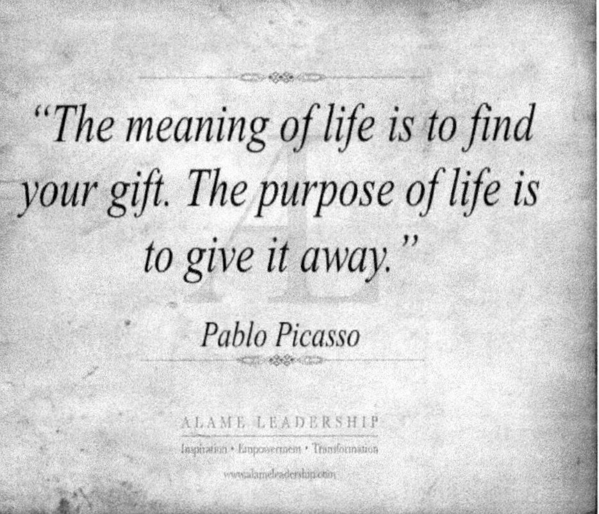
"The meaning of life is to find your gift. The purpose of life is to give it away."

Pablo Picasso

ALAME LEADERSHIP
Inspiration • Empowerment • Transformation
www.alameleadership.com

Efforts and courage are not enough without purpose and direction.

John F Kennedy

QuotePixel.com

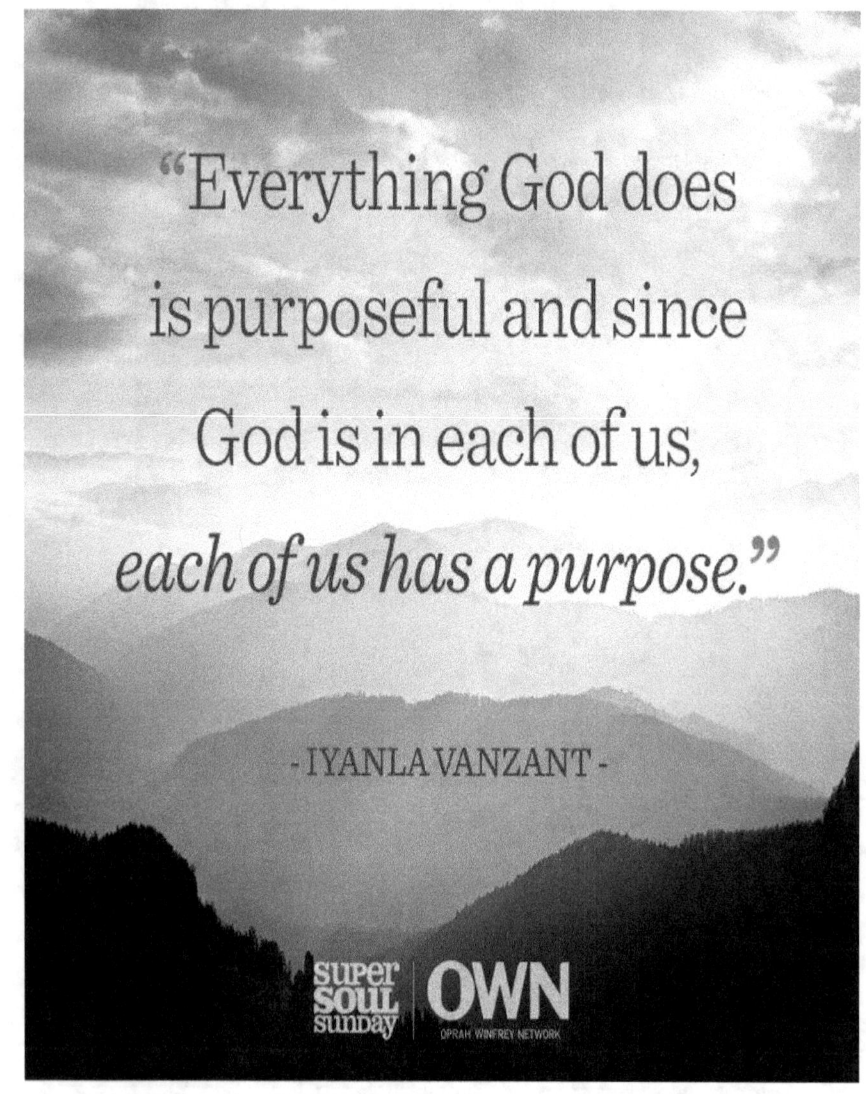

"Everything God does is purposeful and since God is in each of us, each of us has a purpose."
- IYANLA VANZANT -
super soul sunday
OWN
OPRAH WINFREY NETWORK

THE POINT OF PURPOSE IS IN THE PRESENT MOMENT

The point of purpose is in the present moment. The present moment is all there really is. We experience the past, present, and future, now. Our purpose is not yesterday, or tomorrow, our purpose is now. We must do purpose now.

Now is all we have control of. "Nothing has happened in the past; it happened in the Now. Nothing will ever happen in the future; it will happen in the Now." *The past is history, the future is a mystery, but the present is a gift.*

Note these excerpts from Eckhart Tolle, The Power of Now: A Guide to Spiritual Enlightenment:

"Realize deeply that the present moment is all you have. Make the NOW the primary focus of your life."

"Time isn't precious at all, because it is an illusion. What you perceive as precious is not time but the one point that is out of time: the Now. That is precious indeed. The more you are focused on time – past and future – the more you miss the Now, the most precious thing there is."

"Any action is often better than no action, especially if you have been stuck in an unhappy situation for a long time. If it is a mistake, at least you learn something, in which case it's no longer a mistake. If you remain stuck, you learn nothing."

"All negativity is caused by an accumulation of psychological time and denial of the present. Unease, anxiety, tension, stress, worry - all forms of fear - are caused by too much future, and not enough presence. Guilt, regret, resentment, grievances, sadness, bitterness, and all forms

of non-forgiveness are caused by too much past, and not enough presence."

"See if you can catch yourself complaining, in either speech or thought, about a situation you find yourself in, what other people do or say, your surroundings, your life situation, even the weather. To complain is always non-acceptance of what is. It invariably carries an unconscious negative charge. When you complain, you make yourself into a victim. When you speak out, you are in your power. So change the situation by taking action or by speaking out if necessary or possible; leave the situation or accept it. All else is madness."

"As soon as you honor the present moment, all unhappiness and struggle dissolve, and life begins to flow with joy and ease. When you act out the present-moment awareness, whatever you do becomes imbued with a sense of quality, care, and love - even the most simple action."

"Your outer journey may contain a million steps; your inner journey only has one: the step you are taking right now."

Living with purpose in the present moment has immense benefits for our mental, emotional and spiritual health. One of the benefits is that time moves swiftly and we are completely focused on the task at hand. Anyone who has been engrossed in something understands this. It can happen to anyone, at any time, as long as they are doing something that completely fascinates them. Time seems to slow down – or even stop.

It can happen while playing a musical instrument or playing a sport. We are so focused and so concentrated that time flies. This makes us feel alive! It is only a matter of time, and time can only seem long to those who dwell within it without purpose. But to those who dwell in time with purpose, time moves swiftly and brings about this great result.

Mihaly Csikszentmihalyi is a psychologist who has studied the state of total focus while performing an enjoyable activity. He termed this state "Flow." He found that this state occurs across many disciplines and throughout all cultures. It is a distinctive human trait common to all people who are completely focused and living with purpose in the present moment.

According to Csikszentmihalyi, emotions are not just contained and channeled, but positive, energized and life affirming. One cannot be in a state of anxiety or depression while experiencing Flow. No one likes "killing time" and being bored. Deep down, this feeling kills us slowly. Living with purpose is the path to a true life, true contribution and true happiness.

THE PROPHETS OF PURPOSE

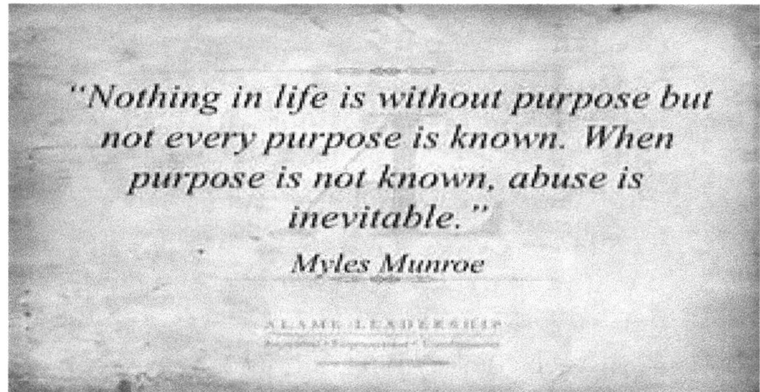

MYLES MUNROE

The late great Myles Munroe was in my opinion the prophet of purpose. Dr. Munroe stated that: "The only thing worse than death, is a life without a reason or purpose." In many of his sermons and writings he posits the idea that the greatest question is not "what," but "why." The greatest thing about what, is why. We must know the why of things. "Why" am I here? Why are we here? Young children often ask the question, "why?"

Dr. Munroe preached in many sermons, that God gave Adam a job and a purpose, before he received a wife. God has created all things with a purpose. The creator of a thing determines its purpose. Purpose is what the creator of a thing has in mind, as the reason for the creation of the thing in the first place. That is the "why", of a thing. If you want to know the purpose of a thing or person, you must ask its creator.

Dr. Munroe in sermons and books makes these six points about purpose.

1. God is a God of purpose.
2. Nothing in this world is without purpose. The roach and the rat have a purpose.
3. Not every purpose is known.
4. Where purpose is not known, abuse is inevitable. Abuse = "abnormal use".
5. If you want to know the purpose of a thing, don't ask the thing.
6. Purpose is the key to fulfillment.

Dr. Munroe makes a powerful point in stating that when purpose is not known, abuse is inevitable. The word abuse means, "abnormal" use". When a person does not know their purpose, they will abuse or misuse themselves. When a man does not know the purpose of a woman, he will misuse even abuse women. Purpose is absolutely fundamental.

I had a purpose before anybody had an opinion about me. You had a purpose before anybody had an opinion about you. If you don't know your purpose, you are probably serving someone else's. If you don't know your purpose, you can be repurposed by someone else.

"Know thyself" (African proverb). "And to thy, self be true." In other words, know your purpose, and to your purpose be true. That is why the African concept of Sankofa (reach back and fetch it) is important. We as African people we must reach back and get our purpose and self-knowledge.

This will allow us as Bob Marley said to: "Emancipate yourselves from mental slavery, none but ourselves can free our minds." A slave has accepted someone else's purpose and culture. You can't be a slave, and an African with the knowledge of self at the same time. You would be a prisoner always looking to escape back to your own purpose. That is why the white supremacist removed the knowledge of self from their Black slaves. We were mis-educated and trained to serve the purpose of White Supremacy.

Purpose must be revealed, and educed out from. We must reach back within our Ancient African culture to rediscover our purpose today. The word education means to "educe out from." A true education educes out the potential and purpose of a person. That is why Carter G. Woodson wrote the book The Mis-Education of the Negro. Making the point that Black Americans were "mis-educated", and "repurposed" to serve White Supremacy. Our full potential is not educed out in the American educational system. We have not been made to realize our God given purpose to glorify and serve God, and ourselves.

When a young man does not know his purpose he will abuse himself, and will be misused by others. The same is true for a young woman. People will "repurpose" you, if you don't know your own purpose. You can't be true to a purpose you are unaware of. As Jesus stated, "My people perish, because of a lack of knowledge."

A slave is someone that has been repurposed by someone else. Instead of serving self, they serve the other that has enslaved them. That is why the knowledge of self and purpose is fundamental. The knowledge of self and purpose will enable one to resist the devil that would abuse or misuse them. The knowledge of self and purpose, is what gives us a strong mental immune system, and will enable us to resist abuse and misuse by others (mental slavery).

Dr. Munroe's last point is that purpose is fundamental and the key to fulfilment. Fulfillment is what Maslow refers to as "self-actualization." To realize my potential and purpose, gives me a sense of fulfillment and peace of mind. Purpose produces fulfillment, peace and contentment of mind.

Purpose leads to ultimate fulfillment and self-actualization. From a seed, to a full bloomed flower. Happiness is a product of purpose, not the object of purpose. There is joy in knowing that you are on purpose, even when you are in the pain and process of purpose.

Circumstances and crises are God's tools to move you into your purpose and the maximizing of your potential. Myles Munroe (The Pain of purpose)

More Quotes by Dr. Myles Monroe

Leadership is the capacity to influence others through inspiration motivated by passion, generated by vision, produced by a conviction, ignited by a purpose. --Myles Munroe

We each were endowed at birth with a unique gift, something we were born to do or become that no one else can achieve the way we can. God's purpose is that we bear abundant fruit and release the blessings of our gift and potential to the world. --Myles Munroe

Purpose gives birth to hope and instills the passion to act. --Myles Munroe

You are not saved for the sole purpose of going to heaven; you are saved to finish your assignment on earth. --Myles Munroe

In life, purpose is defined by the thing that makes you angry. Martin Luther was angry; Mandela was angry; Mahatma Gandhi was angry; Mother Teresa was angry. If you are not angry, you do not have a ministry yet. --Myles Munroe
"The greatest tragedy in life is not death, but a life without a purpose."
— Myles Munroe --- (Prophet of Purpose)

"People generally fall into one of three groups: the few who make things happen, the many who watch things happen, and the overwhelming majority who have no notion of what happens. Every person is either a creator of fact or a creature of circumstance. He either puts color into his environment, or, like a chameleon, takes color from his environment." — Myles Munroe, understanding your potential discovering the hidden you

"When purpose is not known, abuse is inevitable" — Myles Munroe, Understanding The Purpose And Power Of Woman

"You must decide if you are going to rob the world or bless it with the rich, valuable, potent, untapped resources locked away within you." — Myles Munroe, understanding your potential discovering the hidden you

"Ecclesiastes 3:1-2: 'To everything there is a season, …A time for every purpose under heaven.'…If you're having a bad time right now, it cannot last. If you cannot find a job right now – That is only a season. If your business is going in the wrong direction – it's a seasonal slide." – Myles Munroe

Purpose is when you know and understand what you were born to accomplish. Vision is when you see it in your mind and begin to imagine it. Myles Munroe

We were placed on earth to fulfil a purpose, and that purpose is what gives meaning to our lives, you were sent to the world to make an impact and make a difference. Myles Munroe

"One of the greatest tragedies in life is to watch potential die untapped." — Myles Munroe

"Your purpose can be fulfilled only during the time you are given on earth to accomplish it."
— Myles Munroe, The Principles and Power of Vision: Keys to Achieving Personal and Corporate Destiny

"People who changed the world have declared independence from other people's expectations."
— Myles Munroe, The Principles and Power of Vision

The value of life is not in its duration, but in its donation. You are not important because of how long you live, you are important because of how effective you live. Myles Munroe

You weren't born just to live a life and to die; you were born to accomplish something specifically. Matter of fact, success is making it to the end of your purpose; that is success... Success is not just existing. Success is making it to the end of why you were born. Myles Munroe

Death can never kill an idea. Ideas are more powerful than death. Ideas outlive men and can never be destroyed. Myles Munroe

Rick Warren

The most well-known book on purpose is, "The Purpose Driven Life" by Rick Warren. The Purpose Driven Life is designed as a forty day spiritual journey – one chapter a day – with the goal of answering the question "What on earth am I here for?" (p15). The question is broad enough to address both believer and unbeliever alike, which may in part explain the width of its appeal.

Warren's first section serves as a primer to the question. His goal is to prepare the reader to answer the two questions God will pose to him on the last day: What did you do with Jesus, and what did you do with what God gave you (p34)?

Since life is about bringing glory to God (p53), the question to be answered is "How can I bring glory to God?" (p55). The answer is by worshiping Him, loving other believers, becoming like Christ, serving others with our gifts, and telling others about Him (pp55-57).

The remaining five sections flesh out these ideas respectively. The most useful summary is given by Warren himself on p306, working from the Great Commandment (Matt 22:37-40) and the Great Commission (Matt 28:18-20).

1. **"Love God with all your Heart"**: You were planned for God's pleasure, so your purpose is to love God through *worship*.
2. **"Love your neighbor as yourself"**: You were shaped for serving, so your purpose is to show love for others through *ministry*.
3. **"Go and make disciples"**: You were made for a mission, so your purpose is to share God's message through *evangelism*.

4. **"Baptize them into…"**: You were formed for God's family, so your purpose is to identify with his church through *fellowship*.
5. **"Teach them to do all things…"**: You were created to become like Christ, so your purpose is to grow to maturity through *discipleship* (all emphases his).

Worship is not about what pleases us, but about what makes God smile. God smiles when we love, trust, obey, and praise Him, and when we use our abilities for His glory (pp70-76). "The heart of worship is surrender…. Offering yourself to God is what worship is all about" (p78, citing Rom 12:1-2). Since "God wants to be your best friend", Warren gives some practical suggestions for developing that friendship through prayer, meditation, honesty, and obedience (pp85-113).

Fellowship is symbolized by baptism, and designed to teach us how to love (pp117-129). Since the life of a body is contained in the cells, "every Christian needs to be involved in a small group within their church….This is where real community takes place, not in the big gatherings" (p139). Real fellowship is characterized by authenticity, mutuality, sympathy, and mercy (p143). But cultivating this kind of community takes honesty, humility, courtesy, confidentiality, and frequency (pp145-151). It also takes an ability to restore broken relationships and protect the unity of the church (pp152-167).

Discipleship is about "taking on [God's] values, attitudes, and character" (p172). We grow by making good decisions (p174), by allowing God to transform the way we think through His Spirit and our repentance (p182), by abiding in God's word (pp185-192), and by persevering through trouble and temptation (pp192-223).

Ministry is our service to believers (see p281). It is not an optional extra of the Christian life (p233), and it is in large part what gives our lives meaning and significance (pp228, 232). We begin to understand how God means for us to serve when we understand our SHAPE: our Spiritual gifts, Heart, Abilities, Personality, and Experience (p236-256). Yet mature Christian servant-hood realizes that God often calls us to secondary ministries based on "wherever [we're] needed at the moment" rather than on our SHAPE (p257-270).

Evangelism is our service to unbelievers (p281). Fulfilling the evangelistic mandate God has given you will require abandoning your life agenda for God's (p286). But failing to do so will mean wasting your life (p285). Personal evangelism, then, is to be accomplished by sharing your life message, which includes your testimony, your life lessons, your godly passions, and the good news (pp289-295); and it should be accompanied by an increasingly global concern for the unsaved, which is ideally caught by going on a short term missions trip (p304).

Balancing these five purposes is the key to persevering and succeeding in the Christian life. "Blessed are the balanced; they shall outlast everyone" (p305). To achieve that balance, we need to discuss these ideas with others, record our life lessons through the discipline of journaling, and write out a specific life purpose statement that includes each of these five biblical purposes (pp305-319).

Earl Nightingale

The Power of Purpose (Posted Jul 21, 2013 Psychology Today)

In this excerpt from an "Our Changing World" radio broadcast by the late Earl Nightingale, the dean of personal development explains what he called "The Strangest Secret" —and why it is the key to living a successful life.

When we say "nearly five percent of men and women achieve success" then we have to define success. The following is the best definition we've found: "Success is the progressive realization of a worthy ideal."

If a person is working toward a predetermined goal and knows where to go, then that person is successful. If a person does not know which direction they want to go in life, then that person is a failure.

"Success is the progressive realization of a worthy ideal."

Therefore, who succeeds?

The only person who succeeds is the person who is progressively realizing a worthy ideal. The person who says, "I'm going to become this" and then begins to work toward becoming it.

Have you ever wondered why so many men and women work so hard and honestly without ever achieving anything in particular? Why others do not seem to work hard at all and yet get everything? We sometimes think it is the magic touch or pure luck. We often say, "Everything they touch turns to gold." Have you ever noticed that a person who becomes successful tends to continue this pattern of success?

Or on the other hand, how a person who fails seems to continually fail? Well, the answer is simple — those who succeed have established personal goals.

Success is not the result of making money; making money is the result of success and success is in direct proportion to our service.

Here are five steps that will help you realize success:

Have you ever wondered why so many men and women work so hard and honestly without ever achieving anything in particular? Why others do not seem to work hard at all and yet get everything?

1. Establish a definite goal.

2. Stop running yourself down.

3. Do not think of all the reasons why you cannot be successful — instead think of all the reasons why you can achieve success.

4. Trace your emotions back to childhood — discover where you first got the negative idea you would not be successful — face your fears.

5. Renew your self-image by writing a description of the person you want to become — Act the part—You are that person!

George Bernard Shaw said:

"People are always blaming their circumstances for what they are. I don't believe in circumstances. The people who get on in this world are the people who get up and look for the circumstances they want, and if they can't find them, make them."

Well, that is pretty apparent, isn't it? And every person who discovered this believed – for a while – that he was the first one to work it out. We become what we think about.

Now, it stands to reason that a person who is thinking about a concrete and worthwhile goal is going to reach it, because that's what he's thinking about. And we become what we think about.

Conversely, the man who has no goal, who doesn't know where he's going, and whose thoughts must therefore be thoughts of confusion and anxiety and fear and worry, becomes what he thinks about. His life becomes one of frustration and fear and anxiety and worry. And if he thinks about nothing...he becomes nothing.

So decide now. What is it you want? Plant your goal in your mind. It's the most important decision you'll ever make in your entire life. All you've got to do is plant that seed in your mind, care for it, and work steadily toward your goal, and it will become a reality.

How do you begin?

First: It is understanding emotionally as well as intellectually that we literally become what we think about; that we must control our thoughts if we're to control our lives. It's understanding fully that..."as ye sow, so shall ye reap."

Second: It's cutting away all fetters from the mind and permitting it to soar as it was divinely designed to do. It's the realization that your limitations are self-imposed and that the opportunities for you today are enormous beyond belief. It's rising above narrow-minded pettiness and prejudice.

Third: It's using all your courage to force yourself to think positively on your own problems, to set a definite and clearly defined goal for yourself. To let your marvelous mind think about your goal from all possible angles; to let your imagination speculate freely upon many different possible solutions. To refuse to believe that there are any circumstances sufficiently strong to defeat you in the accomplishment of your purpose. To act promptly and decisively when your course is clear. And to keep constantly aware of the fact that you are, at this moment, standing in the middle of your own "acres of diamonds."

And fourth: Save at least 10 percent of every dollar you earn.

It's also remembering that, no matter what your present job, it has enormous possibilities – if, you're willing to pay the price by keeping these four points in mind:

1. You will become what you think about.

2. Remember the word "imagination" and let your mind begin to soar.

3. Courageously concentrate on your goal every day.

4. Save 10 percent of what you earn.

Finally, take action – ideas are worthless unless we act on them.

Nightingale-Conant Corporation subscribe to Nightingale-Conant's Higher Achievement e-newsletter.

T.D. Jakes

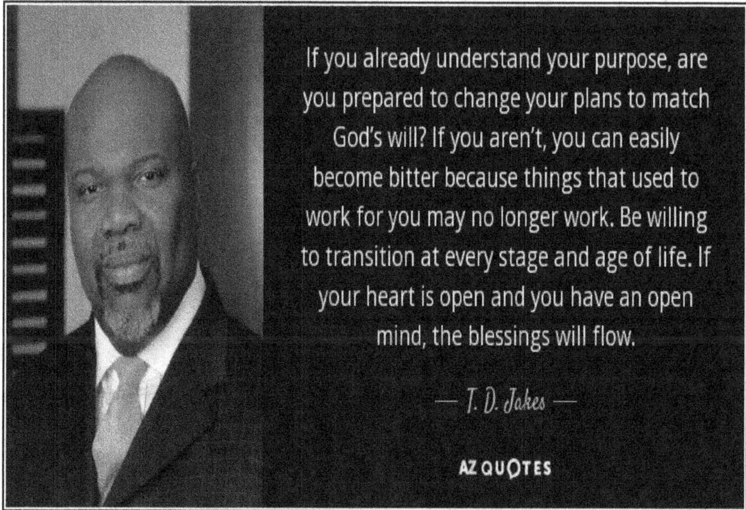

A shining talent like dancing or acting is hard to hide, but a true life purpose can be tougher to identify. "This happens all the time," Oprah says to <u>Bishop T.D. Jakes</u> in a video clip from an episode of "<u>Oprah's Lifeclass:</u> The Tour."

"Anybody who can sing just a little bit, or they can write a piece of a poem, they think they're supposed to be <u>Maya Angelou</u> all of a sudden. And you say people confuse talent with purpose."

Bishop Jakes says that yes, being good at something doesn't mean it's your calling. Pulling from a sermon he preached entitled "Living on Purpose," he says, "You must understand that the purpose is an underlying chemistry that makes you live your life.

"I was sitting on a speaker and I said, 'This speaker will bear the weight of my body. It will make a chair in a pinch,'" he continues. "But it was not designed to be a chair. I am not using it for its highest and best use. Many times we are pushed into functioning in an area that is not our highest and best use because someone needed us to be something we were not created to be."

If you're stuck on how to tell the difference between talent and purpose, Bishop Jakes advises that you look honestly at your best skills. "So many times you have a modicum of talent in an area," he says, "maybe just enough talent to appreciate people who are really called to that area. It doesn't mean that you need to necessarily go out and do that thing."

However, if you're in a situation where your talents aren't being used to the maximum, it could be beneficial in the long run.

"You may start out doing something that was not 'the thing' that you were created to do," says Bishop Jakes. "It may only be the thing that leads to the thing you were created to do. So don't stop at where you are as if it were the destination, when in fact in reality it may be the transportation that brings you into that thing you were created to do."

"Oprah's Lifeclass", airs Sundays on OWN.

T.D. Jakes uses his gift for connecting with people to inspire us to be the best versions of ourselves. He unlocks the door to personal growth not only for the tens of thousands of members of his congregation at The Potter's House in Dallas, Texas, but also for the millions who seek out his wisdom through his books, films, television and social media.

Bishop TD Jakes Talks 'Living With Purpose' on 'Oprah's Lifeclass'

Bishop Jakes appeared on "Oprah's Lifeclass the Tour" to discuss with the iconic talk show host and the show's interactive audience how to live a life of purpose.

Jakes, an influential Christian leader who has a 30,000-member church in Dallas, Texas, is well known for his powerful sermons in which he addresses topics relevant to faith -- such as living a life of purpose.

The minister's hour-and-a-half "Lifeclass" episode was filmed at the Peabody Opera House in St. Louis, Mo. Prior to addressing the audience on his own, Winfrey spoke to Jakes about how he discovered his own life's purpose.

"The first time I walked on a stage I knew that was what I was created to do. I knew that there was a calling and a sense of purpose in my life that gave me fulfillment and a sense of destiny," the pastor said.

Jakes, who started his church at the age of 19, discussed with the talk show host how discovering one's life purpose requires looking beyond feelings of insignificance in order to understand that no life is a mistake and that everyone has been brought to Earth with a master plan for their lives.

"We are here by a divine purpose," he said.

Throughout the episode the pastor shared different challenges people face when determining their life's purpose, including being pushed into functioning in areas that might not be at an individual's highest or best use, confusing talent with purpose, and doing that which one is not created to do.

"Half the battle is not spending your life to be what you aren't," he said, before sharing with the audience that the key to fulfilling their purpose is to find passion.

"It is your passion that empowers you to be able to do that thing you were created to do," Jakes said.

The popular pastor also touched on the need to let go of fear and embrace forgiveness and courage to be able to move forward into a life of purpose.

"Resist your fear, fear will never lead to you a positive end. Go for your faith and what you believe," Jakes said. "Get out of the boat Peter, walk on the water."

Jakes, whose sermons are broadcast both nationally and internationally, did not directly mention Christ during the show, but referenced the Bible when discussing the importance of working hard and making investments in life -- particularly if the returns are not immediately available.

"Be not deceived: God cannot be mocked; for whatsoever a man soweth, that shall he also reap," he said, quoting Galatians 6:7.

Living on purpose, as I define it, is to become aware that we were all created to serve some specific function in life. Some of these purposes might be lofty, attracting the accolades of the world. Some of these purposes may be down-to-earth, such as raising a child, teaching or engaging in some other activity that may not be as acknowledged by society but is still significant.

The pursuit of your life is to come into that purpose. And the waste of your life is to miss that purpose. The problem, though, for most of us is discovering what our purpose is. Here are a few mistakes we make while looking for it, ones that can distract or misdirect us.

For a few years, I was involved in music. I was a choir director, and I played the piano. I noticed that when our choir got ready to sing, people got more blessed out of me introducing the song and talking about the song than they did from the song itself. Gradually I began to realize that the tail was wagging the dog. I love music to this day, and I have a fairly good understanding of music and theory and how they operate. But that's not why I'm here on earth.

Just because you admire something doesn't mean it's your purpose. Don't let yourself be distracted by something that should be a hobby. If you, like me, enjoy music, that doesn't necessarily mean you should be the one directing the song. Buy some CDs or enjoy music on your headset, just don't let it take your focus.

The "But That Drives Me Crazy" Mistake

Usually, when things drive us crazy, we're taught to walk away or ignore them. But sometimes it can help to take a closer look. For example, if somebody does something incorrectly, and their error drives us crazy, we shouldn't criticize the person — we should look at what our inability to tolerate their error can show us. What you cannot stand to see done badly is exactly where you ought to work. If you can't stand it when the church programs are done incorrectly or when the invitations are not sent out in time — if you want things in order — maybe you should consider working in an area of administration.

Other people might not even be bothered by these things, but your inability to put up with anything less than excellence means that you have an interest there. You need to recognize, "This is an area I have passion about."

Sometimes your purpose may be totally opposite to the preparation of your life. It may be that you got a degree in one thing, but it's not fulfilling to you because it's not the thing that you were really created to do. It may be that your family and friends have misdirected you to where they have a need. So your education, your background, your circumstances, your job end up restricting you from finding your fulfillment.

This happened to me. My father owned a janitorial service, and it was his dream for us to own another family business together. As an adult, my brother started a windows-and-siding company and invited me to be a part of it, but when I tried to twist myself into what my family wanted me to be, the business ultimately failed. I had substituted everyone's happiness for my own, trying to live up to my brother's dreams because I loved him and trying to live up to my father's expectations. But in reality, my purpose was in a completely different arena than anything they could have imagined.

This happens to so many of us. Every day at work, you might be like Jonah in the story in Bible, right when the ship hits a storm. Jonah knew, "I'm really going in the wrong direction. I'm going into the mouth of a whale." You know the exact same thing. You have to have the courage to withstand other people's opinions and ideas and to flow into your own purpose.

The lives we lead do not always lend time for inner reflection. We're so busy that we don't make space for prayer, for mediation. We don't really examine. We throw ourselves into this busy-ness so deeply that we don't take the time to pause for even a Sabbath, if you will.

Everything else in creation has a Sabbath — a winter, a season of not being fruitful. But we're afraid of this. Look at fruit trees: They give up the winter for the spring. It's not healthy for livestock to produce all year long. We're so busy spitting out project after project after project that we don't give ourselves a chance to heal and restore and reflect and really find our internal heartbeat.

It can be hard at first to identify that internal heartbeat, but recognizing it determines what will give you fulfillment and gratification. Think of it as an inward applause for every moment where you feel in harmony with yourself, and when you hear it — be it loud and clear or soft and slightly muffled — you'll know exactly what it is and what you're meant to do.

These 10 quotes from Bishop Jakes will inspire you to relentlessly pursue your purpose in life.

1. "Don't stop at where you are as if it were the destination, when in fact, in reality, it may be the transportation that brings you into that thing you were created to do."

Our current circumstances should never limit us from reaching our true potential. We must turn our struggles into the vehicles that spur our transformation.

2. "Everything you've gone through is preparation for what's about to happen in your life. The LORD has already given you a word, MOVE!"

When we "move," we bring about the growth we desire. Tragedy hasn't stopped you, heartbreak didn't defeat you, failure does not define you; use this hard-earned wisdom to grasp your purpose and shape your future.

3. "We need to be who we were called to be instead of contorting ourselves into what other people want us to be!"

The surest way to lose yourself is to focus on other people's voice instead of your own. Jakes calls on us to walk into our destiny and embrace our true purpose in life. Stop conforming!

4. "It is time for us to find the thing we were created to do, the people we were meant to affect, and the power that comes from alignment with purpose."

This powerful quote from his book, "Instinct: The Power to Unleash Your Inborn Drive," speaks to the clarity to be gained from the search for our truth. If you are in a job that drains you, it's time to galvanize your forces and take the necessary steps to move on. The road will be taxing, but the promise of fulfilling your true purpose will fortify your conviction.

5. "Here is the problem with how many people approach the question of purpose: Many are looking outside of themselves for their purpose, destiny, or meaning in life. The very key to knowing your purpose is discovering and celebrating your personal identity."

Purpose resides in us; we must be directors in the script of our lives. In his work "Identity: Discover Who You Are and Live A Life Of Purpose," T.D. Jakes reminds us that as you get to know more about yourself -- your likes, dislikes, values and triggers -- you will have a greater sense of whether or not the life you lead suits you. Life's noise can be deafening; when is the last time you sat in complete silence and listened for the messages from your heart?

6. "God is about to plant you in a big thing. Your eyes have not seen, your ears have not heard, neither has entered into your heart what God has in store for you!"

From his electric sermon, "The Starving Prince," from The Potter's House Sunday service, Jakes challenges us to believe in our purpose. The "big thing" we were meant to do is coming! As you search for your true purpose in life, do not waver in your faith to overcome your current adversity.

7. "If we are called to be the salt of the earth, we have to get out of the saltshaker. Get out of your comfort zone, enlarge your territory."

We are called to embrace change. Turn your tumultuous relationship around, heal the wounds that hold you back, dare to take a step towards your dream career. Your actions will loosen the ties that bind and will move you closer to where you are supposed to be.

8."Your Passion is your conviction about it, your Purpose is why you do it, your Destiny is where you are going."

Passion and purpose are joined at the hip and move together, lock-step, towards destiny. Where there is passion, connect it to your purpose. Then set your goals higher than you think humanly possible. You will find your reward.

9. "At any age you can still ignite your passion through finding your purpose!"

Consider an athlete or a famous musician. They thrive in the skill that defines them, and the energy flow is seamless. We can all tap into our own inner excellence and radiate this same energy. Were you meant to counsel others? Do you have a way with numbers? As Jakes discusses, find your genuine purpose and never settle for false comfort. Ignite your passion and your purpose will reveal itself!

10. "When you know your purpose, you know what isn't your purpose, so you can stop being distracted trying to do something that is not in the wheelhouse of what you were designed to do!"

You need to find the wheelhouse of what you were called to do. T.D. Jakes calls on us to shed our toxic distractions and share our divine spark on a daily basis. He reminds us that as long as we have breath in our bodies, we have the ability to flourish.
(T.D. Jakes.Com)

Dr. Wayne W. Dyer

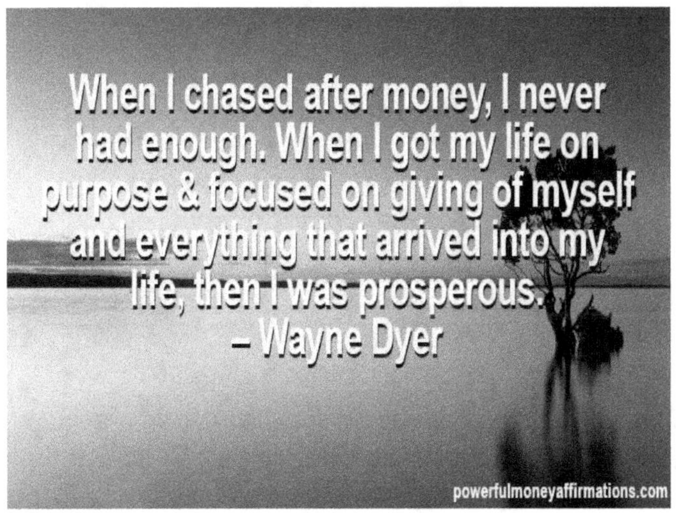

When you are inspired by a great purpose, everything will begin to work for you. Inspiration comes from moving back in-spirit and connecting to the seven faces of intention. When you feel inspired, what appeared to be risky becomes a path you feel compelled to follow. The risks are gone because you are following your bliss, which is the truth within you. This is really love working in harmony with your intention. Essentially, if you do not feel love, you do not feel the truth, and your truth is all wrapped up in your connection to Spirit. This is why inspiration is such an important part of the fulfillment of your intention to live a life on purpose.
Wayne Dyer

The following is an excerpt from, "You Can Heal Your Life.Com (Blog)" Dr. Wayne W. Dyer, 4- 28- 2013

A sense of purpose is at the very top of the pyramid of self-actualization created by Abraham Maslow more than 50 years ago. Through his research, Dr. Maslow discovered that those who feel purposeful are living the highest qualities that humanity has to offer. During the many years I've been in the fields of human development, motivation, and spiritual awareness, this is the topic that more people inquire about than anything else.

I'm repeatedly asked questions such as: *How do I find my purpose? Does such a thing really exist? Why don't I know my purpose in life?* Being on purpose is what the most self-actualized people accomplish on their life journeys. But many individuals feel little sense of purpose, and may even *doubt* that they have a purpose in life.

The very fact of your existence indicates that you have a purpose. The key question for most of us is: "What is my purpose?" And I hear that question in as many forms as there are people wondering about it: *What am I supposed to be doing? Should I be an architect, a florist, or a veterinarian? Should I help people or fix automobiles? Am I supposed to have a family or be in the jungle saving the chimpanzee?* We're befuddled by the endless number of options available to us, and wonder whether we're doing the right thing. I urge you to forget these questions. Move instead to a place of faith and trust in the universal mind, remembering that you emanated from this mind and that you're a piece of it at all times.

In response to the question *What should I do with my life?* I suggest that there's only one thing you *can* do with it, since you came into this life with nothing and you'll leave with nothing: *You can give it away.* You'll feel most on purpose when you're giving your life away by serving others. When you're giving to others, to your planet, and to your Source, you're being purposeful. Whatever it is that you choose to do, if you're motivated to be of service to others while being authentically detached from the outcome, you'll feel on purpose, regardless of how much abundance flows back to you.

Allow yourself to be in the feeling place within you that's unconcerned with such things as vocational choices or doing the things you were destined to do. When you're in the service of others, or extend kindness beyond your own boundaries, you'll feel connected to your Source. You'll feel happy and content, knowing that you're doing the right thing.

I get that feeling of inner completion and contentment that lets me know that I'm on purpose by reading my mail or hearing the comments I so frequently hear when I'm walking through airports or eating at restaurants: *You changed my life, Wayne Dyer. You were there for me when I felt lost.* This is different from receiving a royalty payment or a great review, which I also enjoy. The personal expressions of gratitude are what sustain me in knowing that I'm on purpose.

Outside of my chosen occupation, I feel purposeful in a myriad of ways virtually every single day. When I extend assistance to someone in need, when I take a moment to cheer up a disgruntled employee in a restaurant or store, when I make a child laugh who sits otherwise ignored in a stroller, or even when I pick up a piece of litter and place it in a trash can, I feel that I'm giving myself away and, as such, feel purposeful. Stay focused on giving and your purpose will find you.

Eckhart Tolle

In his book, A New Earth, Eckhart Tolle states that we have both an inner and an outer purpose, according to Tolle. Our outer purpose changes with circumstances and necessarily involves time, whereas our inner purpose remains always the same: It is to be absolutely present in whatever we do and so let our actions be guided and empowered by awareness, the awakened consciousness, rather than controlled by the egoic mind. We fulfill our destiny and realize our purpose when we awaken to who we are: conscious Presence. Most people treat the present moment as if it were an obstacle that they need to overcome. Since the present moment is Life itself, it is an insane way to live.

In awakened doing there is complete internal alignment with the present moment and whatever you are doing right now. The doing is then not primarily a means to an end, but an opening for consciousness to come into this world. Aligning yourself with the Now is aligning yourself with universal purpose, the purpose of the whole. What is the purpose of the whole? The birth and flowering of consciousness. The whole then guides you in whatever you think or do. Tolle explains in A New Earth:

"Awakened doing has three modalities, depending on circumstances and the nature of the activity. They are acceptance, enjoyment, and enthusiasm. If there is neither acceptance, enjoyment, or enthusiasm in what you do, you are out of alignment with universal purpose. You are creating unhappiness, that is to say suffering in one form or another. One way of defining the ego is simply this: a dysfunctional relationship with the present moment. What I refer to as the "new earth" — the outer forms created by awakened doing — arises as more people realize that their purpose is to allow consciousness to emerge through whatever they do.

Tolle continues:

"One thing we can do is to notice the little things all around us, paying attention to details such as the birds in the trees and the flowers in the garden or the park — just notice the beauty everywhere, even the smallest things. To notice seemingly insignificant things requires alertness.

That alertness is the key. It is the unconditioned. It is consciousness itself. Another helpful practice is to watch the breath, and breathe consciously. If we are paying attention to our breath, we cannot be thinking of anything else at the same time. Our attention is in the now moment and not on our worries about yesterday or our plans for what we will do next week.

We are just breathing, not thinking. Because the practice of breath meditation takes us out of the activity of thought, it is an effective way to awaken. In fact, breath, because it has no form as such, has traditionally been equated with spirit, the formless One Life. In the German language, the word atmen, meaning "breathing," is derived from atman, which in Sanskrit, the language of ancient India, refers to the innermost essence or universal self."

Tolle Quotes

"The primary cause of unhappiness is never the situation but your thoughts about it."
— Eckhart Tolle

"The past has no power over the present moment."
— Eckhart Tolle

"Acknowledging the good that you already have in your life is the foundation for all abundance."
— Eckhart Tolle

"Life will give you whatever experience is most helpful for the evolution of your consciousness. How do you know this is the experience you need? Because this is the experience you are having at the moment."
— Eckhart Tolle, A New Earth: Awakening to Your Life's Purpose

"Give up defining yourself - to yourself or to others. You won't die. You will come to life. And don't be concerned with how others define you. When they define you, they are limiting themselves, so it's their problem. Whenever you interact with people, don't be there primarily as a function or a role, but as the field of conscious Presence. You can only lose something that you have, but you cannot lose something that you are."
— Eckhart Tolle

"Sometimes letting things go is an act of far greater power than defending or hanging on."
— Eckhart Tolle

"Realize deeply that the present moment is all you have. Make the NOW the primary focus of your life."

— Eckhart Tolle, The Power of Now: A Guide to Spiritual Enlightenment

"Life is the dancer and you are the dance."
— Eckhart Tolle, A New Earth: Awakening to Your Life's Purpose

"Any action is often better than no action, especially if you have been stuck in an unhappy situation for a long time. If it is a mistake, at least you learn something, in which case it's no longer a mistake. If you remain stuck, you learn nothing."
— Eckhart Tolle, The Power of Now: A Guide to Spiritual Enlightenment

"All negativity is caused by an accumulation of psychological time and denial of the present. Unease, anxiety, tension, stress, worry - all forms of fear - are caused by too much future, and not enough presence. Guilt, regret, resentment, grievances, sadness, bitterness, and all forms of non-forgiveness are caused by too much past, and not enough presence."
— Eckhart Tolle, The Power of Now: A Guide to Spiritual Enlightenment

Brian Tracy

Brian Tracy states that the great tragedy is that most people go through life and die with their music still in them. They react and respond to pressures and events, to parents and to bosses, to bills and responsibilities, and never take the time to sit down and think about what it is that they really want for themselves.

You were put on this earth to do something wonderful with your life. Your job is to find out what that wonderful thing is and then to throw your whole heart into doing it extremely well. Your life may have a single purpose, like that of Mother Theresa of Calcutta, or your life may have multiple, sequential purposes, one after the other as you evolve and grow and develop into a higher and better person.

According to Brian Tracy, the one common characteristic of the most successful men and women is _clarity_. They are absolutely clear about what they stand for and believe in, and where they are going. And you must achieve this <u>clarity</u> as well.

What is your "heart's desire?" Your heart's desire is defined as the one thing that you and you alone were put on this earth to do. It is that something special that you are uniquely suited to do in an excellent fashion. Your job throughout your life is to discover your heart's desire. It is only then that you will be truly happy, completely successful and totally fulfilled. What is yours?

An excerpt from Brian Tracy's "_Goals_"

Your major definite purpose can be defined as the one goal that is most important to you at the moment. It is usually the one goal that will help you to achieve more of your other goals than anything else you can accomplish. It must have the following characteristics:

1. It must be something that you *personally* really want. Your desire for this goal must be so intense that the very idea of achieving your major purpose excites you and makes you happy.

2. It must be clear and specific. You must be able to define it in words. You must be able to write it down with such clarify that a child could read it and know exactly what it is that you want and be able to determine whether or not you have achieved it.

3. It must be measurable and quantifiable. Rather than "I want to make a lot of money," it must be more like "I will earn $100,000 per year by (a specific date)."

4. It must be both believable and achievable. Your major definite purpose cannot be so big or so ridiculous that it is completely unattainable.

5. Your major definite purpose should have a reasonable probability of success, perhaps fifty-fifty when you begin. If you have never achieved a major goal before, set a goal that has an 80 percent or 90 percent probability of success. Make it easy on yourself, at least at the beginning. Later on, you can set huge goals with very small probabilities of success and you will still be motivated to take the steps necessary to achieve them. But in the beginning, set goals that are believable and achievable and that have a high probability of success so that you can be assured of *winning* right from the start.

6. Your major definite purpose must be in *harmony* with your other goals. You cannot want to be financially successful in your career on the one hand and play golf most of the time on the other. Your major definite purpose must be in harmony with your minor goals and congruent with your values.

" CLARIFY YOUR PURPOSE

What is the *why* behind everything you do?
When we know this in life or design
it is very empowering
and the path is clear."

— Jack Canfield

Your Life has PURPOSE.
Your Story is IMPORTANT.
Your Dreams COUNT.
Your Voice MATTERS.
You Were Born To Make
AN IMPACT.

www.MesmerizingQuotes.com

<u>**Nia** (nee-AH) = **Purpose**</u>

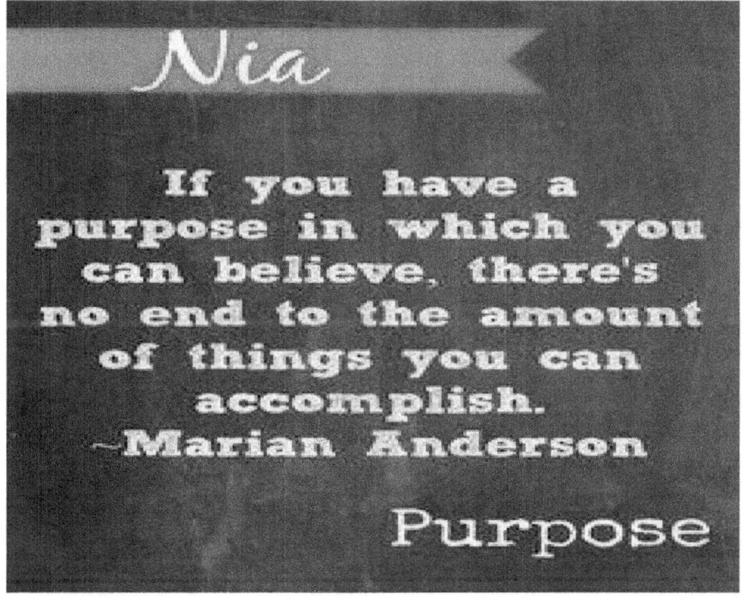

"To make our collective vocation the building and developing of our community in order to restore our people to their traditional greatness."

The fifth principle of the Nguzo Saba is Nia, which is essentially a commitment to the collective vocation of building, developing and defending our national community, its culture and history in order to regain our historical initiative and greatness as a people.

The assumption here is that our role in human history has been and remains a key one. That we as an African people share in the grand human legacy Africa has given the world. That legacy is one of having not only been the fathers and mothers of humanity, but also the fathers and mothers of human civilization, i.e., having introduced in the Nile Valley civilizations the basic disciplines of human knowledge. It is this identity which gives us an overriding cultural purpose and suggests a direction. This is what we mean when we say we who are the fathers and mothers of human civilization have no business playing the cultural children of the world. The principle of Nia then makes us conscious of our purpose in light of our historical and cultural identity.

Inherent in this discussion of deriving purpose from cultural and historical identity is a necessary reference to and focus on generational responsibility. [Frantz] Fanon has posed this responsibility in competing terms. He says, "each generation must, out of relative obscurity, discover its mission, [and then] fulfill it or betray it" (48).

The mission he suggests is always framed within the larger context of the needs, hopes and aspirations of the people. And each of us is morally and culturally obligated to participate in creating a context of maximum freedom and development of the people.

Finally, Nia suggests that personal and social purpose are not only non-antagonistic but complementary in the true communitarian sense of the word. In fact, it suggests that the highest form of personal purpose is in the final analysis, social purpose, i.e., personal purpose that translates itself into a vocation and commitment which involves and benefits the community. As we have noted elsewhere, such a level and quality of purpose not only benefits the collective whole, but also gives fullness and meaning to a person's life in a way individualistic and isolated pursuits cannot.

For true greatness and growth never occur in isolation and at other's expense. On the contrary, as African philosophy teaches, we are first and foremost social beings whose reality and relevance are rooted in the quality and the kinds of relations we have with each other. And a cooperative communal vocation is an excellent context and encouragement for quality social relations. Thus, [W.E.B.] Du Bois' stress on education for social contribution and rejection of vulgar careerism rooted in the lone and passionate pursuit of money is especially relevant.

For again our purpose is not to simply create money markers, but to cultivate men and women capable of social and human exchange on a larger more meaningful scale, men and women of culture and social conscience, of vision and values which expand the human project of freedom and development rather than diminish and deform it.
Practice **Nia** every day!

NIA
PURPOSE
To restore African American people to their traditional greatness.
To be responsible to Those Who Came Before (our ancestors)
and to Those Who Will Follow (our descendants).

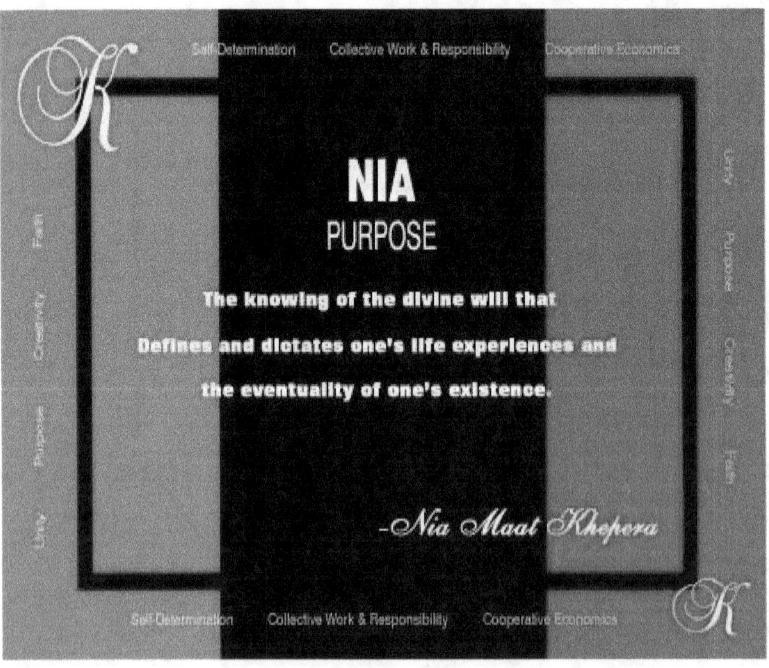

Self-Determination   Collective Work & Responsibility   Cooperative Economics
NIA
PURPOSE
The knowing of the divine will that
Defines and dictates one's life experiences and
the eventuality of one's existence.
-Nia Maat Khepera
Self-Determination   Collective Work & Responsibility   Cooperative Economics
Unity   Purpose   Creativity   Faith

123 THE PROCESS OF PURPOSE

NIA! PURPOSE without it how would we survive.
Why without it not a dream, nor vision nor scribe
would be alive.

Nia! the fifth night of Kwanzaa, our people have
always searched for it. Some found it in Freedoms
redemptive song, on with the Civil Rights Movement
and then they just moved along.

Shuffling their feet in an endless beat of apathy
Drinking cheap wine and smoking rock and losing
all sense and sensibility!

No purpose and the people become as the undead.
No idea of what occurred behind them and no direction
to lead them ahead.

NIA! Harambee...Habari gani!
What is your purpose, to have the phat ride
with the flyest girl inside. No thought of college
and no neighborhood pride.

Nia! What is your purpose, to have more things
than Mr. And Mrs. Jones, and their closet full of dry
bones! Nia find ya purpose and your ancestors
live on.

BJS(C)2002 msluciousb,

Definite Major Purpose (DMP)

Napoleon Hill's much acclaimed book **Think and Grow Rich** begins.

"Thoughts are things," and powerful things at that, when they are mixed with definiteness of purpose, persistence, and a BURNING DESIRE for their translation into riches, or other material objects."

You need to know where you are headed before you start walking. You need to know your **Definite Major Purpose** (DMP).

Understanding and defining your **DMP** will enable you to live how you want to live. No amount of self-help books and inspirational stories can inspire you to bring a change unless you don't know what the change you seek actually is.

"A man without a definite major purpose is as helpless as a ship without a compass." – Napoleon Hill

How Do You Define Your Definite Major Purpose?

Your DMP is the ultimate goal that you wish to achieve in your life. It could be money, success in business, healthy relationships etc. etc. Your Definite Major Purpose is yours to define, and that's exactly what you need to be working on achieving. Your DMP, once determined, will become the central mission of your life and will make it easier to set goals and achieve them.

Goals don't do much on their own, except become milestones to a road unknown. DMP will help you achieve freedom, fulfillment, inspiration and recognition. Following

are a few questions that you will need to ask in order to define your **Definite Major Purpose** in life:
Here are some questions that can help you define your DMP (From Jason and Jeremy of <u>Internet Business Mastery Academy</u>):

- Why am I here?

- What is the top purpose of my life?

- What are the most important things I want to accomplish in my life?

- What fulfils me above all other things?

Below are a few more questions you can answer to get a broader view of what you eventually want to achieve all the professional and personal success for:

The Million Dollar Question
- What would you do if you had a million dollars in the bank?

- In what ways would your life change?

- What would you do differently?

- What are the things that you would want to purchase in the course of a year with that money?

- What three goals do you think you would be able to accomplish with that money?

<u>Bruce Lee – My Definite Chief Aim</u> (20th July 2016 by Lak Loi)

Bruce Lee studied profound philosophers, both past & present. One such philosopher, was Dr. Napoleon Hill (26 Oct 1883 – 8 Nov 1970), who wrote the bestseller book 'Think & Grow Rich'. He presented the idea of a "Definite Major Purpose" or "Chief Definite Aim" as a challenge to his readers in order to make them ask themselves, "In what do I truly believe?" According to Hill, 98% of people had few or no firm beliefs, and this alone put true success firmly out of their reach.

Bruce wrote the following "Chief Definite Aim" — at which time Bruce would have been 28 years of age and a minor TV star in the United States, having featured in a number of shows which included, most notably, the ill-fated Green Hornet series. With his second child recently born and no financial security to speak of, the clearly determined founder of Jeet Kune Do decided to put his "Definite Chief Aim" down on paper.

(Transcript) **My Definite Chief Aim**

I, Bruce Lee, will be the first highest paid Oriental super star in the United States. In return I will give the most exciting performances and render the best of quality in the capacity of an actor. Starting 1970 I will achieve world fame and from then onward till the end of 1980 I will have in my possession $10,000,000. I will live the way I please and achieve inner harmony and happiness.

Bruce Lee 1969

Bruce Lee died on 20 July 1973 at the young age of 32 years, 2 weeks before the release of his blockbuster movie 'Enter the Dragon'. After Bruce's death, 'Enter the Dragon' catapulted Bruce Lee into a superstar, not only in the USA, but worldwide. 'Enter the Dragon' grossed over $25 million in the US alone.

My Definite Chief Aim

I, Bruce Lee, will be the first highest paid Oriental super Star in the United States. In return I will give the most exciting performances and render the best of quality in the capacity of an actor. Starting 1970 I will achieve world fame and from then onward till the end of 1980 I will have in my possession $10,000,000. I will live the way I please and achieve inner harmony and happiness.

Bruce Lee
Jan. 1969

How to Create Your Definite Chief Aim

"Would you tell me please, which way I ought to go from here?"
asked Alice. "That depends a good deal on where you want to get
to," replied the Cat. - Lewis Carroll, Alice in Wonderland.
c
The key elements of a Definite Chief Aim:

1)   The main goal/achievement that you want to accomplish, be specific as possible and make it the ultimate dream/goal all your other goals lead up to.

2)   What you are willing to give up or give in return to achieve your main goal

3)   Your three to four smaller secondary goals that will make your primary goal a reality.

   You want to write it in the present tense with all your goals starting with "I will" or "I am". Make it short enough to fit on one sheet of paper and make sure to place it somewhere you can see it throughout the day.

   Your goal is to develop the habit of reading your goal at least 3 times a day and preferably more, as often as you can. Remember, your mind accomplishes what you think about the most. So you should develop the habit of saying it out loud with emotion as soon as you wake up, during the day and again right before you go to bed.

   You take advantage of Auto Suggestion (planting the idea in your subconscious mind) and your subconscious mind then takes the goals and puts them in the forefront of your mind. The more you repeat your Definite Chief Aim with emotion, the more you build belief and a burning desire to accomplish whatever you set your mind to. The two operative words in that sentence were: belief and desire. They are the 2 keys to you doing what you need to do and achieving the goals you set for yourself.

As Napoleon Hill writes in "The Law Of Success In Sixteen Lessons": the subconscious mind may be likened to a magnet, and when it has been vitalized and thoroughly saturated with any definite purpose it has a decided tendency to attract all that is necessary for the fulfillment of that purpose.

He goes on to write: Until a man selects a definite chief aim in life, he dissipates his energies and spreads his thoughts over so many subjects and in so many different directions that they lead not to power, but to indecision and weakness.

Once you have clarity about what you want and why you want it, you're ready to follow these steps to attain your Definite Chief Aim:

1) Write a Clear Description of your Definite Chief Aim. Years ago, before Arnold Schwarzenegger had made his mark on Hollywood, he stated his Definite Chief Aim: "I am going to be the number-one box-office star in all of Hollywood." Explaining how he intended to accomplish this feat, he said: "What you do is create a vision of who you want to be, and then live into that picture as if it were already true." In 1991, receipts from Terminator II confirmed Schwarzenegger to be the most popular box office draw in the world, thus successfully accomplishing his Definite Chief Aim.

2) Include a Clear Statement of What You Intend to Give in Return. As I'm sure you agree, there's no such thing as something for nothing. To get what you want, it's important to decide what you will give in return. Oprah's Definite Chief Aim has been to make a positive difference in the lives of millions of people. "As far back as I can recall," she says, "my prayer has been the same: Use me, God. Show me how to take who I am, who I want to be, and what I can do, and use it for a purpose greater than myself."

Oprah has achieved phenomenal success for herself and others by focusing on a purpose greater than herself.

3) Believe You Can and Will Attain Your Definite Chief Aim. What you attain is limited only by your capacity to believe you can have it. To believe you can have what you want, keep thinking thoughts of having what you want. Magnetize your mind with positive affirmations. Visualize, imagine and feel yourself already in possession of your desire. In 1987, Jim Carrey was a struggling comic and part-time dishwasher, dreaming of fame and fortune. In addition to affirmations and visualizations, he wrote himself a check for $10 million and dated it Thanksgiving 1995, adding the notation "for acting services rendered." In the fall of 1995, he did in fact reach his Definite Chief Aim when he signed a $10 million contract to film "The Mask."

4) Take Inspired Action. Tune in to guidance and inspiration from your Non-Physical Partner. When you listen to your inner voice and follow the guidance you receive, you are truly co-creating with Source. You don't have to do it all alone. Your intuition will lead you step by step in the direction of your Definite Chief Aim.

5) Persevere. To accomplish your Definite Chief Aim, you must stay the course. If your Definite Chief Aim is based on a burning desire for its achievement, you will be able to persevere through doubts and difficulties. Remember that the dominating thoughts of your mind WILL transform themselves into physical reality. Thomas Edison had a Definite Chief Aim to create the electric light bulb. He persevered through 10,000 failed attempts before successfully realizing his dream.

"If you don't have a dream, how you gonna have a dream come true?" – (From the movie, South Pacific)

Vitalize and thoroughly saturate your mind with your Definite Chief Aim. Concentrate on the end result as you see and feel and believe yourself already in possession of it. Your Definite Chief Aim is a blueprint that will lead you, step by step, toward its attainment. It's a bridge between your dream and your reality.

Napoleon Hill told readers in his 1937 classic, "Think and Grow Rich," that it was an absolute must for them to have their major purpose in life written down and to read this statement on a daily basis with real passion and conviction.

The user of the DCA had to write down.

- The sum of money they desired
- The date by which they wanted to attain it
- The service they were prepared to give in return for these riches

Daily repetition of this statement would then create the desire and belief needed to follow through with a plan for acquiring mass riches.

- The power is in the *purpose*. It doesn't matter what your chief aim is, you just need to have one. It could be finding love, creating a successful business and yes, acquiring a certain sum of money.
- It's got to be *bold*. There is no room for timidity when creating a DCA. You need something that is going to motivate you and unless it challenges your present reality it's unlikely to do so (look back over Bruce Lee's if you need guidance here).
- It will change. Don't worry about creating the perfect DCA that will stay with you until old age. Circumstances and events will change but it's important to remember that a person with a purpose *always* has a focus which they can move towards.

Napoleon Hill told readers in his 1937 classic, <u>Think and Grow Rich</u>, that it was an absolute must for them to have their major purpose in life written down and to read this statement on a daily basis with real passion and conviction.

The user of the DCA had to write down.

- The sum of money they desired
- The date by which they wanted to attain it
- The service they were prepared to give in return for these riches

Daily repetition of this statement would then create the desire and belief needed to follow through with a plan for acquiring mass riches.

- The power is in the *purpose*. It doesn't matter what your chief aim is, you just need to have one. It could be finding love, creating a successful business and yes, acquiring a certain sum of money.
- It's got to be *bold*. There is no room for timidity when creating a DCA. You need something that is going to motivate you and unless it challenges your present reality it's unlikely to do so (look back over Bruce Lee's if you need guidance here).
- It will change. Don't worry about creating the perfect DCA that will stay with you until old age. Circumstances and events will change but it's important to remember that a person with a purpose *always* has a focus which they can move towards.

Bruce Lee's DCA is taken from the book, <u>Bruce Lee: Fighting Spirit</u>, by Bruce Thomas

Steps excerpt from, "The Magic of a Definite Chief Aim" , by Kate Corbin

MA'AT

"Two tendencies govern human choice and effort, the search after quantity and the search after quality. They classify mankind. Some follow Maat, others seek the way of animal instinct." — KMT Proverb

Maat or **Ma'at** was the ancient Egyptian concept of truth, balance, order, law, morality, and justice. Maat was also personified as a goddess regulating the stars, seasons, and the actions of both mortals and the deities, who set the order of the universe from chaos at the moment of creation. After her role in creation and continuously preventing the universe from returning to chaos, her primary role in Egyptian mythology dealt with the weighing of souls (also called the weighing of the heart) that took place in the after world Her feather was the measure that determined whether the souls (considered to reside in the heart) of the departed would reach the paradise of afterlife successfully. Pharaohs are often depicted with the emblems of Ma'at to emphasize their role in upholding the laws of the Creator.

Written at least 2,000 years before the Ten Commandments of Moses, the 42 Principles of Ma'at are one of Africa's, and the worlds, oldest sources of moral and spiritual instruction. Ma'at, the Ancient Egyptian divine Principle of Truth, Justice, and Righteousness, is the foundation of natural and social order and unity. Ancient Africans developed a humane system of thought and conduct which has been recorded in volumes of African wisdom literature, such as, these declarations from the Book of Coming Forth by Day (the so-called Book of the Dead), The Teachings of Ptah-Hotep, the writings of Ani, Amenemope, Merikare, and others

The heart of the deceased was believed to be the seat of the soul and it was weighed on the scale of *Maát,* against a feather, which represented the principles of truth and righteousness (the seven cardinal virtues). This symbolic weighing of the heart against the feather of truth *(Maát)* was performed to establish the righteousness of the deceased. The scale of Maát was balanced after the recitation of the "42" Declarations of Innocence or Admonitions of Maát.

The 42 Divine Principles of Ma'at

1. I have not committed sin.
2. I have not committed robbery with violence.
3. I have not stolen.
4. I have not slain men or women.
5. I have not stolen food.
6. I have not swindled offerings.
7. I have not stolen from God/Goddess.
8. I have not told lies.
9. I have not carried away food.
10. I have not cursed.
11. I have not closed my ears to truth.
12. I have not committed adultery.
13. I have not made anyone cry.
14. I have not felt sorrow without reason.
15. I have not assaulted anyone.
16. I am not deceitful.
17. I have not stolen anyone's land.
18. I have not been an eavesdropper.
19. I have not falsely accused anyone.
20. I have not been angry without reason.
21. I have not seduced anyone's wife.
22. I have not polluted myself.
23. I have not terrorized anyone.
24. I have not disobeyed the Law.
25. I have not been exclusively angry.
26. I have not cursed God/Goddess.
27. I have not behaved with violence.
28. I have not caused disruption of peace.
29. I have not acted hastily or without thought.
30. I have not overstepped my boundaries of concern.
31. I have not exaggerated my words when speaking.
32. I have not worked evil.
33. I have not used evil thoughts, words or deeds.
34. I have not polluted the water.

35. I have not spoken angrily or arrogantly.
36. I have not cursed anyone in thought, word or deeds.
37. I have not placed myself on a pedestal.
38. I have not stolen what belongs to God/Goddess.
39. I have not stolen from or disrespected the deceased.
40. I have not taken food from a child.
41. I have not acted with insolence.
42. I have not destroyed property belonging to God/Goddess

(From *"Book of Coming Forth By Day or The Egyptian Book of the Dead,"* as edited by E.A. Wallis Budge)

The *Neophyte* or students ultimate aim in Kemet (Egypt) was for a person to become "one with God" or to "become like God." The path to the development of godlike qualities was through the development of virtue, but virtue could only be achieved through special study and effort.

7 Principles of MAÁT

Truth
Justice
Harmony
Balance
Order
Reciprocity
Righteousness/Propriety

To decolonize the African mind, African freedom-seekers must destroy their deeply rooted, interconnecting networks of internalized European or Arab values and beliefs. These are the invisible chains of mental slavery that for centuries have allowed Europeans and Arabs to manipulate and control them, first as slaves and religious converts, and now as pseudo-citizens. Sankofa practice is an indispensable weapon in the war to decolonize or re-Africanize the African mind.

SANKOFA

In order for Africans in American, and all over the world, to know their true purpose, we must practice Sankofa. We were not created to be slaves or be inferior to white people. Carter G. Woodson in his famous book, The Mis-Education of the Negro, makes the point that we were mis-educated, and our true God given purpose and potential was not cultivated. In order to know our true purpose as African people, we must reach back before slavery and claim our original God given purpose.

Sankofa can mean either the word in the Akan language of Ghana that translates in English to " reach back and get/fetch it" (san - to return; ko - to go; fa - to look, to seek and take) or the Asante Adinkra symbols of a bird with its head turned backwards taking an egg off its back, or of a stylized heart shape.

The egg represents our culture and African history. The egg for the bird represents its past, present, and future. Without an understanding of our past, we are lost in the present, and unprepared for the future. We must practice Sankofa, we must reach back and get it.

Reach back and get "our-story." "His-story" (slave-master's) mis-educates us. The winner of the war tells the story of what happened, not the loser.

We can't expect those who enslaved us and their children who continue to profit from our ignorance to tell our story with truth. It would incriminate them. We must take the responsibility to tell "our-story." The Honorable Elijah Muhammad stated: "that if a man won't treat you right, what would make you think that he would teach you right?" "The same people that enslaved us will never send you a teacher that will free you from their grip."

Beyond what our children learn in public and "their" private schools, our community and parents must take the responsibility to teach after school and summer programs. The "focus" must be on basic skills and thinking skills enrichment. Equally important is that there be a heavy component of African history (our-story) and culture. We must reach back and get it (Sankofa).

The successful ethnic groups in America and the world have all done this. Jews, Chinese, Japanese, and African groups, such as The Nation of Islam, have organized around a cultural base to produce academic excellence. We would do well to follow these examples. We do not have to convert to a religion or try to become another race.

"Whether to be African or not to be (Hilliard)?" Is the fundamental question. Everything flows from this. We are African, or we are nothing as far as our collective African liberation is concerned. So let's reach back and get our Black African spiritual principles that European's stole from us and white washed. That would be "true" liberation theology.

Purpose Quotes

"The purpose of life is to live mindfully and passionately in the present moment, to love unabashedly, to be a lifelong learner, to seek adventure and growth, and to spread kindness and peace along the way."   Barrie Davenport

<u>Joshua Becker</u>: *"The purpose of life is to give it away in the service of others."*

<u>Brendan Baker</u>: *"The purpose of life is to make a difference (a positive difference!)."*

<u>Gary Vaynerchuk</u>: *"To leave Legacy that is a North Star for all my family in the future."*

<u>Will Mitchell</u>: *"The purpose of life is self-actualization – shaping the world in our vision through reaching our full potential."*

<u>Christie Marie Sheldon</u>: *"The only Soul-Filled purpose of life is to love and let what makes you soulfully happy guide you — it'll all work out if that's your guiding force."*

Emerson says: *"The purpose of life is not to be happy. It is to be useful, to be honorable, to be compassionate, to have it make some difference that you have lived and lived well."*

"Let yourself be silently drawn by the strange pull of what you really love." ~Rumi

"Real success is not rooted in positions, places or possessions, but in fulfilment of God's purposes for our lives."
— Ifeanyi Enoch Onuoha

"Did you ever notice that all machines are made for some reason?" he asked Isabelle. "They are built to make you laugh, like the mouse here, or to tell the time, like clocks, or to fill you with wonder like the automaton. Maybe that's why a broken machine always makes me a little sad, because it isn't able to do what it was made to do." Isabelle picked up the mouse, wound it again, and set it down. "Maybe it's the same with people," Hugo continued. "If you lose your purpose...it's like you're broken."
— Brian Selznick, The Invention of Hugo Cabret

"Discover a purpose that gives you passion. Develop a plan that makes you persistent. Design a preparation and motivates you to optimize your potentials. Do it because you love it!"
— Israelmore Ayivor, Dream Big!: See Your Bigger Picture!

"Purpose and passion - purpose is what will guide you to your best self and the passion will keep you there."
— Nikki Rowe

"They plan, and Allah plans. Surely, Allah is the Best of planners." #Quran 8:30

"I'm not unhappy," he said. "Only people with no purpose are unhappy. I've got a purpose."
— Cassandra Clare, City of Bones

"God created us for this: to live our lives in a way that makes him look more like the greatness and the beauty and the infinite worth that he really is. This is what it means to be created in the image of God."
— John Piper

"Intelligence minus purpose equals stupidity."
— Toba Beta, Master of Stupidity

"Finding the center of strength within ourselves is in the long run the best contribution we can make to our fellow men. ... One person with indigenous inner strength exercises a great calming effect on panic among people around him. This is what our society needs — not new ideas and inventions; important as these are, and not geniuses and supermen, but persons who can "be", that is, persons who have a center of strength within themselves."
— Rollo May, Man's Search for Himself

"Without God, life has no purpose, and without purpose, life has no meaning. Without meaning, life has no significance or hope."
— Rick Warren, The Purpose Driven Life: What on Earth Am I Here for?

"It is common to represent a title, but inspiring to represent a purpose."
— T.F. Hodge, From Within I Rise: Spiritual Triumph Over Death and Conscious Encounters with "The Divine Presence"

"How to win in life:
1 work hard
2 complain less
3 listen more
4 try, learn, grow
5 don't let people tell you it can't be done
6 make no excuses"
— Germany Kent

"It's not enough to have lived. We should be determined to live for something."
— Winston S. Churchill

"Our sole purpose on this earth is to add value to others. It doesn't make sense to just exist in people's lives or to be a drain on them, does it?"
— Rob Liano

"Don't put your purpose in one place and expect to see progress made somewhere else."
— Epictetus, Discourses and Selected Writings

"Depend on it. God's work done in God's way will never lack God's supply. He is too wise a God to frustrate His purposes for lack of funds, and He can just as easily supply them ahead of time as afterwards, and He much prefers doing so."
— James Hudson Taylor

"Of all the questions I have asked my readers this is the most important: What would you do if you weren't afraid? When you finally give wings to that answer then you have found your life's purpose."
— Shannon L. Alder

"...But we also believe that part of our mission in life is to find our bliss and follow it. Life is a precious and delicate gift. How much of that gift do we squander out of fear?"
— Dianne Sylvan, The Body Sacred

"Man is here for the sake of other men - above all for those upon whose smiles and well-being our own happiness depends."
— Albert Einstein

"Figure out your passion. What floats your boat, rings your bell, lights your tree? A life without passion is possible, but not desirable. Have you really lived at all if you have not lived with passion? Without it would a masterpiece be possible? I don't think so. With purpose, cause and passion, there is no way the end you envision will not become the reality you live."
— Toni Sorenson

"Your purpose is your why."
— Deborah Day

"The most fortunate of us, in our journey through life, frequently meet with calamities and misfortunes which may greatly afflict us; and, to fortify our minds against the attacks of these calamities and misfortunes should be one of the principal studies and endeavors of our lives. The only method of doing this is to assume a perfect resignation to the Divine will, to consider that whatever does happen, must happen; and that, by our uneasiness, we cannot prevent the blow before it does fall, but we may add to its force after it has fallen. These considerations, and others such as these, may enable us in some measure to surmount the difficulties thrown in our way; to bear up with a tolerable degree of patience under the burden of life; and to proceed with a pious and unshaken resignation, till we arrive at our journey's end."
— Thomas Jefferson

"Occupy your thoughts with purpose and you will be so busy pursuing a meaningful future there will be no time for doubt, chaos and disappointment."
— Carlos Wallace, The Other 99 T.Y.M.E.S: Train Your Mind to Enjoy Serenity

"Once you start recognizing the truth of your story, finish the story. It happened but you're still here, you're still capable, powerful, you're not your circumstance. It happened and you made it through. You're still fully equipped with every single tool you need to fulfill your purpose."
— Steve Maraboli

"The crowning fortune of a man is to be born to some pursuit which finds him employment and happiness, whether it be to make baskets, or broadswords, or canals, or statues, or songs."
— Ralph Waldo Emerson

"When we fulfill our function, which is to truly love ourselves and share love with others, then true happiness sets in."
— Gabrielle Bernstein, May Cause Miracles: A 40-Day Guidebook of Subtle Shifts for Radical Change and Unlimited Happiness

"The purpose of life is the expansion of happiness."
— Deepak Chopra

"The only purpose of our lives consists in waking each other up and being there for each other."
— Johanna Paungger, Moon Time: The Art of Harmony with Nature and Lunar Cycles

"REFLECTIONS OF TRUTH

Where you find Truth
Is where you find your reflection
And where you find your reflection
Is where you find love
And where you find love
Is where you find light
And where you find light
Is where you find faith
And where you find faith
Is where you find purpose
And where you find purpose
Is where you find happiness
And where you find happiness
Is where you find Truth
And when you find Truth
Truth will set you free."

— Suzy Kassem, Rise Up and Salute the Sun: The Writings of Suzy Kassem

"The secret of happiness: Find something more important than you are and dedicate your life to it." — Daniel C. Dennett

"The key is for you to discover what you love to do, what you were created to do, and then do it for the people around you with love. That is the abundant life, dear girl, no matter where in the world you live." — Robin Jones Gunn, Finally and Forever

"A man without a definite major purpose is as helpless as a ship without a compass." – Napoleon Hill

"He who has a why to live for can bear almost any how." — <u>Friedrich Nietzsche</u>

"If you have a strong purpose in life, you don't have to be pushed. Your passion will drive you there." — <u>Roy T. Bennett</u>, <u>The Light in the Heart</u>

"If you hang out with chickens, you're going to cluck and if you hang out with eagles, you're going to fly." — <u>Steve Maraboli</u>, <u>Unapologetically You: Reflections on Life and the Human Experience</u>

"Your purpose in life is to find your purpose and give your whole heart and soul to it"
— <u>Gautama Buddha</u>

"Nothing is more creative... nor destructive... than a brilliant mind with a purpose."
— <u>Dan Brown</u>, <u>Inferno</u>

"A writer - and, I believe, generally all persons - must think that whatever happens to him or her is a resource. All things have been given to us for a purpose, and an artist must feel this more intensely. All that happens to us, including our humiliations, our misfortunes, our embarrassments, all is given to us as raw material, as clay, so that we may shape our art."
— <u>Jorge Luis Borges</u>, <u>Twenty-Four Conversations with Borges: Interviews by Roberto Alifano 1981-1983</u>

"Cat: Where are you going?
Alice: Which way should I go?
Cat: That depends on where you are going.

Alice: I don't know.
Cat: Then it doesn't matter which way you go."
— Lewis Carroll, Alice in Wonderland

"The purpose of life is not to be happy — but to matter, to be productive, to be useful, to have it make some difference that you lived at all."
— Leo Rosten

"Those who have failed to work toward the truth have missed the purpose of living."
— Gautama Buddha

"My value as a woman is not measured by the size of my waist or the number of men who like me. My worth as a human being is measured on a higher scale: a scale of righteousness and piety. And my purpose in life-despite what fashion magazines say-is something more sublime than just looking good for men." — Yasmin Mogahed, Reclaim Your Heart: Personal Insights on Breaking Free from Life's Shackles

"Make your work to be in keeping with your purpose" — Leonardo da Vinci

"Great minds have purpose, others have wishes. Little minds are tamed and subdued by misfortunes; but great minds rise above them." — Washington Irving

"Dedicate yourself to what gives your life true meaning and purpose; make a positive difference in someone's life."
— Roy T. Bennett

"Sometimes it takes a wrong turn to get you to the right place."
— Mandy Hale, The Single Woman: Life, Love, and a Dash of Sass

"Find a purpose to serve, not a lifestyle to live."
— Criss Jami, Venus in Arms

"Here is a test to find out whether your mission in life is complete. If you're alive, it isn't."
— Lauren Bacall

"You've been given the innate power to shape your life...but you cannot just speak change, you have to LIVE change. Intent paired with action builds the bridge to success. You can't just want it; you have to do it, live it...BE it! Success isn't something you have, it's something you DO!"
— Steve Maraboli

"Find the thing you want to do most intensely, make sure that's it, and do it with all your might. If you live, well and good. If you die, well and good. Your purpose is done"
— H.G. Wells

"The purpose of life is not to be happy. It is to be useful, to be honorable, to be compassionate, to have it make some difference that you have lived and lived well." — Ralph Waldo Emerson

"The purpose of life is to live it, to taste experience to the utmost, to reach out eagerly and without fear for newer and richer experience."
— Eleanor Roosevelt

"It does not matter how long you are spending on the earth, how much money you have gathered or how much attention you have

received. It is the amount of positive vibration you have radiated in life that matters," — <u>Amit Ray</u>, <u>Meditation: Insights and Inspirations</u>

"The purpose of life is to contribute in some way to making things better." — <u>Robert F. Kennedy</u>

"The purpose of life is a life of purpose." — <u>Robert Bryne</u>

"Everything in this world happens with a purpose. You are born in this world with a purpose, you are chosen by purpose." — <u>Udai Yadla</u>, <u>A Walk in the Rain</u>

"Your feelings and emotions are your strongest indicator if your life is moving in a purposeful direction or not, so listen closely to how you feel" — <u>Rebecca Rosen</u>, <u>Awaken the Spirit Within: 10 Steps to Ignite Your Life and Fulfill Your Divine Purpose</u>

"Occupy your thoughts with purpose and you will be so busy pursuing a meaningful future there will be no time for doubt, chaos and disappointment." — <u>Carlos Wallace</u>, <u>The Other 99 T.Y.M.E.S: Train Your Mind to Enjoy Serenity</u>

"Imagine as if the sole purpose of life is for imagination. Act as if the purpose of life is to realize those imaginations." — <u>Debasish Mridha</u>

"When you find your path in life and are in sync with your primary missions in this lifetime, everything else just falls into place." — <u>Paul O'Brien</u>, <u>Great Decisions, Perfect Timing: Cultivating Intuitive Intelligence</u>

"My main purpose in life is to do everything on purpose." — <u>Efrat Cybulkiewicz</u>

"Without purpose, we're zombies aimlessly roaming the earth." — <u>Ahmed Mostafa</u>

"Step out on faith and walk into your purpose." — Germany Kent

"God will do everything possible to help you, to prepare you for what he had called you to do."
— Sunday Adelaja

"For every purpose there is a plan"
— Sunday Adelaja

"I believe the main purpose of life is to accept with gratitude what you've been blessed with so that you may use those gifts to mold yourself into the best person you can possibly be. Learning to discern things of true value from those of little or no worth is part of the process."
— Richelle E. Goodrich, Smile Anyway

Life without a purpose is like an unsharpened pencil; it has no point."
— Eraica Chan

"The great and glorious masterpiece of man is to live with purpose."
— Michel de Montaigne

The purpose of human life is to serve, and to show compassion and the will to help others. Albert Schweitzer

I truly believe that everything that we do and everyone that we meet is put in our path for a purpose. There are no accidents; we're all teachers - if we're willing to pay attention to the lessons we learn, trust our positive instincts and not be afraid to take risks or wait for some miracle to come knocking at our door. Marla Gibbs

The purpose of human life is to serve, and to show compassion and the will to help others. Albert Schweitzer

Our prime purpose in this life is to help others. And if you can't help them, at least don't hurt them. Dalai Lama

```
In the end, only three things
matter: how much you loved,
how gently you lived, and
how gracefully you let go of
things not meant for you.

-Buddha
```

"Keep away from people who try to belittle your ambitions. Small people always do that, but the really great make you feel that you too, can become great. When you are seeking to bring big plans to fruition, it is important with whom you regularly associate. Hang out with friends who are like-minded and who are also designing purpose-filled lives. Similarly be that kind of a friend for your friends."

Mark Twain

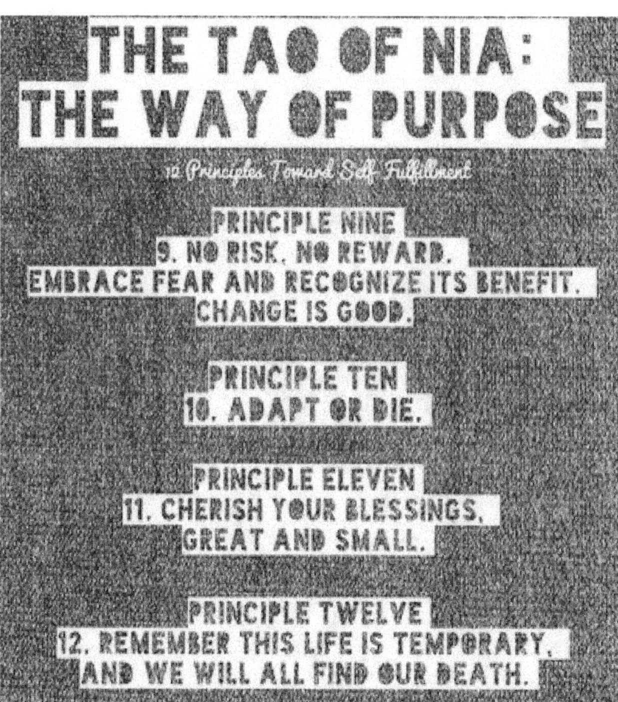
THE TAO OF NIA:
THE WAY OF PURPOSE
12 Principles Toward Self Fulfillment
PRINCIPLE NINE
9. NO RISK, NO REWARD.
EMBRACE FEAR AND RECOGNIZE ITS BENEFIT.
CHANGE IS GOOD.
PRINCIPLE TEN
10. ADAPT OR DIE.
PRINCIPLE ELEVEN
11. CHERISH YOUR BLESSINGS,
GREAT AND SMALL.
PRINCIPLE TWELVE
12. REMEMBER THIS LIFE IS TEMPORARY,
AND WE WILL ALL FIND OUR DEATH.

Everything on Earth
has a purpose, every
disease an herb
to cure it, and
every person a
mission. This
is the Indian Theory
of Existence.
~Morning Dove Salish

"Purpose dictates design. Design hints at purpose.
Who you are as an individual is your design. Now, work out your purpose." Dr Moses Simuyemba
Moses Chikoti Photography

"When you walk in purpose, you collide with destiny."
- Ralph Buchanan

"Have a purpose in life, and having it, throw into your work such strength of mind and muscle as God has given you."
— Thomas Carlyle

"He who has a why to live for can bear almost any how."
— Friedrich Nietzsche

"Nothing is more creative... nor destructive... than a brilliant mind with a purpose."
— Dan Brown

"If you have a purpose in which you can believe, there's no end to the amount of things you can accomplish."
- Marian Anderson

THE FIRST PRINCIPLE OF ETHICAL POWER IS PURPOSE... BY PURPOSE, I DON'T MEAN YOUR OBJECTIVE OR INTENTION-SOMETHING TOWARD WHICH YOU ARE ALWAYS STRIVING. PURPOSE IS SOMETHING BIGGER. IT IS THE PICTURE YOU HAVE OF YOURSELF-THE KIND OF PERSON YOU WANT TO BE OR THE KIND OF LIFE YOU WANT TO LEAD.

KENNETH BLANCHARD

"If your life is cloudy
and you're far, far off course,
you may have to go on faith for a while,
but eventually you'll learn that every time
you trust your internal navigation system,
you end up closer to your right life."

☯ MARTHA BECK

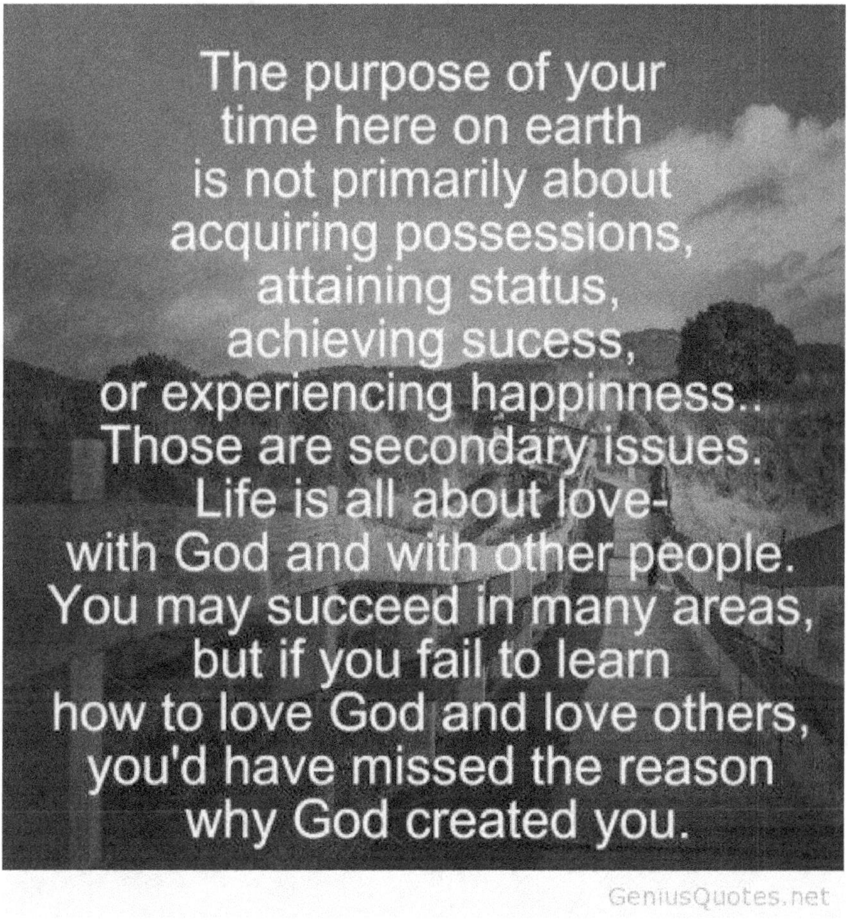

The purpose of your
time here on earth
is not primarily about
acquiring possessions,
attaining status,
achieving sucess,
or experiencing happinness..
Those are secondary issues.
Life is all about love-
with God and with other people.
You may succeed in many areas,
but if you fail to learn
how to love God and love others,
you'd have missed the reason
why God created you.

GeniusQuotes.net

Selected Bibliography

Chamberlain, K., & Zika, S. (1988). Measuring meaning in life: An examination of three scales. *Personality and Individual Differences, 9,* 589-596.

Crumbaugh, J. C. (I 968). Cross-validation of Purpose in Life Test based on Frankl's concepts. *Joumal of lndividual Psychologv, 24,* 74-81.

Crumbaugh, J. C., & Maholick, L. T. (1964). An experimental study in existentialism: The psychometric approach to Frankl's concept of noogenic neurosis. *Journal of Clinical Psychology, 20,* 589-596.

DuRant, R. H., Getts, A., Cadenhead, C., Emans, S. J., & Woods, E. R. (1995). Exposure to violence and victimization and depression, hopelessness, and purpose in life among adolescents living in and around public housing. *Developmental and Behavioral Pediatrics, 16,* 233-237.

Kass, J. D., Friedman, R., Leserman, J., Caudill, M., Zuttermeister, P. C., & Benson, H. (1991). An inventory of positive psychological attitudes with potential relevance to health outcomes: Validation and preliminary testing. *Behavioral Medicine, 17,* 121-129.

Newcomb, M. D., & Harlow, L. L. (I 986). Life events and substance use among adolescents: Mediating effects of perceived loss of control and meaninglessness in life. *Journal of Personality and Social Psychology, 51,* 564-577.

Ryff, C. D. (I989). Happiness is everything, or is it? Explorations on the meaning of psychological well-being. *Joumal of Personality and Social Psychology, 57,* 1069-1081.

Ryff, C. D., & Keyes, C. L. M. (I 995). The structure of psychological well-being revisited. *Journal of Personal and Social Psychology, 69,* 719-727.

Seeman, M. (I 991). Alienation and anomie. In J. P. Robinson, P. R. Shaver, & L. S. Wrightsman (Eds.) *Measures of personality and social psychological attitudes, Volume I* (pp. 291-37 1). San Diego, CA: Academic Press.

Spence, S. A., & Holliman, D. (1995). Exploring the relationship between purpose in life and African American adolescents' use of prenatal care services. *Social Work in Health Care, 22,* 43-53.

Zika, S., & Chamberlain, K. (1992). On the relation between meaning in life and psychological well-being. *British Journal of Psychology, 83,* 133-145.